D0815152

Get Balanced, Get Blissed

Nourishment for Body, Mind and Soul

LYNNE GOLDBERG

Balboa Press books may be ordered through booksellers or by contacting:

Balboa Press
A Division of Hay House
1663 Liberty Drive
Bloomington, IN 47403
www.balboapress.com
1 (877) 407-4847

Printed in the United States of America.

ISBN: 978-1-4525-8259-7 (sc)
ISBN: 978-1-4525-8261-0 (hc)
ISBN: 978-1-4525-8260-3 (e)

Library of Congress Control Number: 2013917192

Balboa Press rev. date: 10/09/2013

Table of Contents

Introduction

I woke up from a terrible dream.

In it, my mother was dying of cancer. She couldn't eat, and her tumor was pressing on a nerve, causing her to cry out in terrible pain. I tried to give her something to eat, but she just looked at me helplessly. In my dream state, I said, "I love you mommy, and I can help you this time. I know what we're supposed to do now."

When I woke up, I realized why I had to write this book. It might be too late for my mom, but my motivation had never been stronger to help others avoid the same pain and suffering that I watched her endure.

I couldn't stand feeling so helpless as I watched someone I loved suffer. I also hated how confusing all the health advice was. People claimed that if we just stopped eating fat, carbs or whatever else was unfashionable at the time, we would be ok. I heard meditation was healthy too, but I didn't know why. So of course, I didn't really believe it.

As I dealt with my own issues of infertility, I can't tell you how many times people told me that if I would just relax, it would work out—that my stress was causing my body to prevent conception.

So much advice, but so few facts. I had heard about holistic health, but I didn't really know what it meant. What was this mind-body-soul thing that people were talking about? And what did I care about the environment as long as my own were safe and taken care of? Selfish, yes, but that's how I really thought at the time. What did I understand about the importance of relationships and how they affect your health?

My mom and I were both out of balance in our lives. She had used food as a way to soothe herself. I used work to escape. She overate to the point that she became obese. I jumped on and off planes to escape from whatever I didn't want to face. A meal for me was a Snickers bar or some crackers with half a bottle of wine, grabbed in a hurry from an airport kiosk. As long as I kept myself busy, I could keep from really feeling.

But contrary to how it may feel sometimes, humans are designed to be in balance. Our bodies naturally and intuitively seek homeostasis whenever we get a little off-kilter. Think about it: when you go into a sauna, you start to sweat. Your body intuitively knows to cool itself. Our bodies are *filled* with that kind of inner wisdom, and tapping into that in order to regain our balance and bliss is what this book is all about. We are designed to enjoy ultimate health and happiness, so who's to say we don't get out there and reclaim our sass and spunk? It's our God-given right!

Bliss: Your Natural State

Bliss. Don't you just love that word? It feels like cotton candy on the tongue, and tickles the ears in a world full of downers like recession, depression, global warming and "Real Housewives" anything. Just typing it makes me happier. And really, that's what bliss is all about—happiness, delight, pleasure, paradise, ecstasy.

If it's a new word to you, or at least a dusty one, that's because we don't talk about bliss much anymore. With so many out of a job or with obesity, type 2 diabetes or other food-related diseases on the rise, with unhealthiness and unhappiness the norm rather than the exception, maybe it's because we feel too guilty being blissful. I'd like to change all that for you. Because bliss is not just a human emotion but a human *right.*

Believe it or not, right now, your body is full of the hormones, signals and capacities to achieve and enjoy that sometimes elusive emotion. If it feels as though that can't possibly be true, don't worry—I'll show you exactly how to uncover your body's natural blissfulness.

So, how did a stressed out Gucci-toting Jimmy-Choo-teetering business CEO find herself teaching meditation? Yoga was for hippies, or so I thought, but when one of my girlfriends dragged me kicking and screaming to a yoga retreat under the guise that I would "lose a few pounds" and "get into shape," I went.

I giggled when we hugged and "namaste-d" one another, and when I found out I couldn't drink or have meat, I literally had to be restrained from leaving the hotel. To say that I was a "natural" at all this would be worse than a lie! But then a weird thing happened: I went from counting off the minutes in meditation as a form of torture to finding that I actually welcomed the peace and tranquility it had to offer.

Never one to "swallow the Kool-Aid" without checking the ingredients first, I began to study. I read a lot of Deepak Chopra's books and found that they touched me deeply. I enrolled in his courses and decided to become a teacher. Along the way, I started experimenting with vegetarianism. I knew I felt better when I didn't eat meat, but I got *really* edgy when I watched gruesome PETA videos.

Then someone handed me a copy of *The China Study,* by Dr. T. Colin Campbell. The study that the book is based on, which covers data from a 20-year joint project between Cornell University, Oxford University and the Chinese Academy of Preventive Medicine, is considered to be the "most comprehensive study of nutrition ever conducted." Researchers surveyed the eating habits of 6,500 adults from all over China and Taiwan and found a correlation between diet and disease.

The book introduced me to something known as the "Diseases of Affluence." As our cultures have gotten wealthier and more adept at mass-producing cattle and chickens, we have been able to feed our families more and more animal protein—which, to the best of our knowledge, was thought to be good for growing children, healthier for our bones and better for overall health.

In fact, what Dr. Campbell found was that "Children who ate the highest protein diets were the ones most likely to get liver cancer." In a series of experiments conducted with rats, he also found that by reducing the amount of animal protein from 20 percent to 5 percent, he could essentially "turn off" cancer cells. In another group of rats, every animal that consumed 5 percent protein avoided cancer—as he put it, "leaving no doubt that nutrition trumped chemical carcinogens."

At first I thought it couldn't possibly be true. I mean, how come I didn't know about it? But the more I read, the more I needed to know. And the more I learned, the more convinced I became that everything I thought I'd known about life, health and happiness was *wrong*. I set out to find the truth and learned more than I ever expected. Much more. Enough, I discovered, to fill a book.

This book is about un-learning all the myths we've been taught, and re-discovering our inner peace and happiness—or, as I call it, that bliss—that's been eluding us for so long.

Are you ever angry for no reason? Do you curse random strangers because there is no bliss in your life? Is your marriage in trouble because you can't kiss with your teeth permanently gritted? This book can help with all that.

Bliss is not a luxury, it's a right. Contrary to how our society can sometimes make us feel, it's *okay* to be happy, to find joy and smile in the face of hardship. In fact, as you'll find in this book, bliss is absolutely necessary for total health—body, mind and soul.

The good news is, it's not so much about *discovering* bliss as *rediscovering* it. Every one of us has that happiness and joy inside; it's actually our natural state. If you need proof, just look at a newborn baby. Its default setting is happiness: gurgling, smiling and cooing, babies are eager to live, learn, grow, and above all, smile. The fact is, we are all born happy, we just lose touch with those instincts somewhere along the way. Get Balanced, Get Blissed is a simple process designed to help you uncover the bliss that's already there.

Just like tending a garden, finding and maintaining bliss in your life is a long-term mission. Despite the beauty of the flowers you've planted, there will always be weeds that need pulling, bugs that need poaching and difficult weather to contend with. But how you deal with those inevitable challenges is what makes your garden different from everybody else's.

Uncovering our bliss is a personal and self-empowering process. No one can take away that inner peace and joy that you'll discover. As we explore the six critical elements needed for balance and bliss, we can take back our inner power and create a life of health and well-being—physically, mentally and spiritually. By focusing on the following steps, we can cultivate more bliss on a regular basis:

- **Part 1:** *Get Blissed:* We've got to start somewhere. No matter where you are, no matter what you're currently struggling with, I'm right there with you. Perfection is not needed on this journey towards rediscovering your bliss. You are ready right now! Come learn about my journey and why I needed so desperately to uncover my own bliss.
- **Part 2:** *Your Body*: The fact is, our bodies are a function of the care we provide for them. Making healthy, nourishing food choices as well as engaging in regular exercise allows us to live better, happier and longer.
- **Part 2:** *Your Mind*: Our minds are incredibly powerful, and never more so than when it comes to the undeniable link between our physical bodies and what's going on in our head. Research supports this link, and frankly, you probably already know it, too. Just think back to the last time you were stressed, mentally burned out or just depressed. Didn't your body feel physically weak, sore or painful as well? As we learn to turn inwards and access our inner stillness, we create wellness in our bodies. As we become aware of our repetitive thoughts and recognize our patterns, we discover that real change is possible—and in fact, necessary—to evolve into a more healthy, blissful state.

- **Part 3:** *Your Environment*: If you've ever walked down a dirty, noisy, polluted city street and felt almost angry as a result, then you already know this undeniable truth: our environment is undeniably tied to our health. One tree has enough oxygen for two people. Our food grows from the soil of the earth, and the water we drink comes from the streams, rivers and lakes all around us. Harming them is like harming ourselves.
- **Part 4:** *Your Relationships*: Healthy relationships feed our soul and allow us to take chances, give love and receive it—while unhealthy relationships only feed our addiction to chocolate-covered cherries eaten in bed, while we use the pages of a trashy novel to wipe chocolate off our faces. Developing strong, meaningful relationships keeps our minds and bodies healthy and serves as our much-needed support system.
- **Part 5:** *Your Spirit*: I'm not talking about team spirit here, the kind you had to sit through for hours on end during all those high school pep rallies. No, our Spirit—our *true* Spirit—is the essence of our being. Sounds kinda weird, I know, but as you develop a connectedness to what's *in*side yourself as well as outside, only then can you start to live truly blissfully.
- **Part 6:** *The Get Blissed 21-Day Challenge*: For those that want to continue with me after the book, the 21-day challenge will supply you with all the tools you'll need to succeed—recipes, meal plans, guided meditation videos and more. Your goals are my goals, and I'm here to help you succeed no matter what. Don't worry, I've got your back! If you're curious, you can check it out on the website at any time, at *LiveBlissNow.com*.

As you can see, rediscovering your bliss isn't as simple as popping a pill, listening to a lecture or going to yoga class. And you won't find it in the pages of a magazine, on the grocery store shelves, online or at the bottom of a wine glass (sorry ladies!). The fact is, bliss is something you uncover, not something you buy, wear, swallow or chug.

We have a lot of fun, rewarding work to do before bliss reveals itself, so if you're ready, willing and able, the first step begins on the very next page. Get excited!

Part 1

Get Blissed

You might think that as the author of a book about bliss, my life—and my body—have always felt blissful. In fact, nothing could be further from the truth.

A Really Bad Year

It was December in Montreal—cold, gray and completely deserted. There were few people on the street and even fewer in the hospital, which is where I sat, hoping not to give birth at only 24 weeks. It had been a long road to get here: years of infertility (IVF, to be exact) treatments slowly depleting our savings accounts, and yet still so much time spent wishing for a pink dot on all those over-the-counter home pregnancy tests.

When I was rushed to the hospital two days prior with contractions, I was admitted into labor. My doctor put me on drugs to slow down my labor and hoped that I could hold out for two more days—when, he explained, the babies would be "viable."

Perhaps his definition of "viable" differed from mine. The thought of giving birth to two beautiful twin girls who might be born with, according to the doctor, underdeveloped lungs, possible blindness, the potential for deafness and so many other potential birth defects, made me literally shake with fear. How could I possibly take care of two precious babies with so many health problems? The prospect seemed not only daunting, but overwhelming and perhaps even impossible.

My career as the vice president of a retail chain, which until that point had been my pride and joy, had already been sidelined by the two-month bed rest. I conducted whatever business I could from my bedroom, but as I was unable to travel to meetings, meet with vendors or do my job in any meaningful way, I was admittedly pretty useless.

As much as I so desperately wanted the twins to hang in there and become truly 'viable,' I prayed they would either arrive now or sit tight for a couple more months. If it happened before 25 weeks, which was two days from now, there would be no life support. The burden of my decision would be lifted. I willed myself to control the situation, but the more I tried, the more obvious it became that I had no control whatsoever. This was out of my hands.

I saw my parents peek into my hospital room. My father, normally so powerful, started to cry when he saw me. My mother, always there to make everything better, always so strong, wrapped her arms around me like a little girl. I felt so guilty. She had just been diagnosed with colon cancer. Her holiday out of the cold and snow was what she needed more than anything, and yet she had interrupted it just to take care of me. Still, I was so relieved she was here. I could relax. There would be someone else to share my burden. Now, I wouldn't have to be so strong.

My husband sighed with relief. He, too, felt she could make it better. My mother sprang into action. She started researching side effects of the steroids they were going to give me, but she was already too late. When the doctor arrived, she checked me and said the words I had been fearing most: "Your water broke, and you have an infection. We will have to deliver them shortly."

My mother looked at me with sympathy and rubbed my arm to comfort me. She was compassionate but unable to change the outcome. I was more practical, my businesswoman side coming out as usual. "Can you give me something for the pain?" I asked.

I refused to engage in any sort of "what if." I decided I would not cry. I tried to keep it together. When I was dilated enough, I lay an unwilling participant as the room transformed. My table grew stirrups, and I watched numbly as the first baby was born. She was whisked away and wrapped and swaddled. A student doctor began to cry. Having weighed all my options, having made up my mind, I had decided not to use life support. Whatever would happen, would happen.

It was all but certain the babies would die. Everyone in the room knew it, I just had to live it. Twenty minutes later, the second baby was born. The babies were brought to me, but I resisted holding them. Too small by far, I didn't even want to see them. Their eyes were closed. I kissed them a final goodbye.

The epidural wore off, and I just wanted to go home. I tried to stand on my own, but my muscles had atrophied from lying in bed for so long. I walked from the room using a cane. *My body has betrayed me again,* I thought to myself as my family followed me out of the hospital. This seemed like the final insult in a punishing series of events that had left me weak, hopeless, pitiful.

Back home, I peered at my breasts in the shower. My milk had already started to come, and it ran down my body with the water. The tears started as well. I feared they would never end.

Bad Things Happen

The hardest thing about being vulnerable is when you realize that bad things can, and inevitably will, happen to you. I had lived a fairly uneventful life until I got pregnant, at which point everything changed. It was hard not to feel cursed after that, or at least damaged. My bright and shiny view of the world had changed forever, but it took time to unravel completely.

Six weeks after coming home from the hospital, I flew to Frankfurt on business. I was used to these trips and usually enjoyed the excitement of the travel. As I began to cross the jetway onto the plane, however, I suddenly froze. I tried to remember the superstition about which foot to use. Should it be my right or left? Tears slid down my cheeks when I couldn't remember. I forced myself onto the plane in anger. Embarrassed by my lack of professionalism and uncontrollable emotions, I scolded myself, hoping no one had noticed how ridiculous I was acting.

Sitting there on the plane, I started making deals with God. "If you let us land safely," I promised desperately, "I will be more charitable." Then, "If you let my mother be okay, I will never gossip again." Part of me knew what I was doing was irrational, but I struggled to get some element—any element—of control.

I struggled with the loss of the twins very differently than my husband had. I wanted to throw myself into finding a solution to our infertility; he wanted to absorb the loss and recover.

As he mourned, I grew impatient. I was sick of hearing about hope and faith, or our names for the babies. I was sad because I missed our future with them; he grieved their loss as if they had already been a part of our lives. I worried because I wanted my mother to see me settled and happy with a baby before she passed away. He wanted to make sure we knew what we wanted before we continued. Should we adopt or try IVF again?

At work I was a zombie. Sitting at my desk, I would make phone calls to lawyers, adoption agencies, doctors and anyone I could think of that could help us make sense of our lives. The choices we had were endless: private or public adoption, surrogates, fertilization. Ultimately the question became: Which lawyer should we use? There was one well-known lawyer in Manhattan that we heard could "get babies quickly." I called.

"What do you want?" he barked when I finally got through.

I whispered, scared to hear his answer: "You come highly recommended. Is it true you can help us adopt in 6 months?"

"Yes," he replied, "but I need 50,000 dollars deposited to my account before I will work with you."

"My mother is sick," I explained. "I don't know how much time we have. Do you have any available birth mothers right now?"

"Lady," he shrieked in his nasal-y New York accent, "Everyone is desperate, get me the money and we'll tawk."

I hung up revolted, shaking and questioning my judgment. Should I just do what he asked and send him the money? By stalling, by questioning, would I be too late? My instinct told me to let it go, so I did.

Work was a distraction, a place I could go where the topic of babies was off-limits, and I could feel like I had at least some control over the rest of my life. As I sat in my office, people buzzed around me with questions, needing my input and approval, handing me paperwork. My opinions mattered here. I had a purpose again, and it felt good. Here, I was valued for what I had accomplished, not whether I could bear children.

Even so, I worked sporadically. I would get a burst of energy, accomplish a great deal and then get sidetracked. My phone rang one day; it was my mother. "I'm worried about you," she said. "I think you are depressed. Maybe you could take some time off," she suggested delicately. "Your brothers are complaining about your work."

I was in a family business. My father, two brothers and I all worked together in a dysfunctional mess. From birth, the three of us kids had all vied for attention from our parents in one form or another. A family business was just an extension of that. So not only was I failing on that front, but suddenly I had also become a financial liability.

Shortly after the call with my mother, my brother approached me tentatively.

"We need to hire someone to replace you," he said. "You are going to be on maternity leave sometime soon anyway when you have your baby. Mummy is sick and could use someone to help her." He paused before adding, "Would you help us train someone?"

I stewed. *How dare they? I had given my heart and soul to this company, and because I forgot a few deadlines, messed up a few times, that was it? I was out?*

How come men could have babies and not have to give up anything? I wondered to myself. *Why was I expected to take care of my mother? What about my father, my brothers?*

Then fear kicked in. *How will I support myself? What will I do for money?* I was a businesswoman. My identity was so closely wrapped up in my career that when I learned it was over, I felt like I was losing everything. I had failed at being a mother and now a career woman—even a good daughter. I couldn't do these few, simple things. So what *was* I good for?

Grief is exhausting. So is worry. My anxiety became so debilitating that I lost whatever energy I had leftover for work, home, my husband, life… anything. At a certain point, it was easier to give up than continue to fight. I took a leave of absence from work and started training someone to take over for me. Then my apathy turned into rage.

I was angry at my brothers. *How could my own family do this to me?*

I was angry at life. *How could God let this happen to me?*

I felt like everything was black and futile. Other people's happiness drove me crazy. I seethed in jealous rage. Anybody complaining about their kids could send me into a catatonic state. How dare they complain about birthday parties and kids' cliques? I would have done anything for a child, no complaints necessary.

As I began caring for my mother, I drew strength from her courage. She never complained. She handled her death sentence with grace and dignity. She wanted to live her life to the fullest in the time that she had left. She went back to school to get a degree in couples counseling, knowing full well there was a strong possibility she would die before it was completed.

She wanted to travel. Even if it meant wearing a catheter and a morphine pump, my mother wanted to go on a safari before she died.

Wanting to squeeze every last ounce of life's pleasures, she went to Africa alongside friends.

My father, knowing she was dying and fearful of being alone, began having an affair. Lying alone in the hospital, my mother would wait for visits, and often he would not come. She befriended the nurses instead and found comfort from everyone else.

As a psychologist, she would listen for hours to people's stories, offering words of support and comfort. Her friends visited regularly. And her children were always around. We were very angry with our father. My mother, the one who had been so wronged, understood and forgave him. She didn't waste time on bitterness and anger. She saw his weakness, and with compassion, she comforted him as he grieved and mourned his loss.

The only bright spot during this time was the formal adoption of our son Josh, who thankfully my mother got to see before she died. And die she did. At the end, she was peaceful, loved and happy.

Meanwhile, I lived. I had no job, my mother had just died and my marriage was collapsing. I was angry, depressed and felt like I had no identity. Taking care of my mother had become my new job. Now I felt like I had nothing. I learned, however, that just the opposite was true.

Your Body, Your Mind, Your Life

What was the purpose of that story? Why share with you all those sad and intimate moments of my life? To reiterate this: we all share something very important—the human condition.

We have all suffered from life's disappointments. We have all had our share of pain, heartache and grief. That's inevitable. As you read my story, I'm sure you nodded your head in understanding. Even if the details were different, you have no doubt experienced pain that has left a mark on you.

One of the most amazing abilities we have is to take those painful moments and use them to learn and grow. I watched someone I loved dearly, die. She was in a tremendous amount of pain and suffered enormously. I have spent a great deal of time learning how to help others avoid what she went through, and I hope that the information I share can help in some way.

Although I didn't understand it at the time, I had been given a *gift*. As I began rebuilding my life, I was able to see the joy in starting over. I had reached rock bottom—been there and back—and now found myself staring at a blank slate. What an opportunity to start over, to create a life that instead of giving me grief and pain, would give me bliss.

I began a new path, followed new instincts and made new friendships, connections and allies. Along the way, I learned some amazing tools to make the process easier. I am offering the words and wisdom in this book in the hopes that when life is dark, you too will have a ray of light to guide you through. No matter how dark it gets, there is always light! Sometimes, you just have to learn how to uncover it.

Live Bliss

Have you ever considered what makes a life happy? Meaningful? Taken one step further, have you ever thought about what can allow us to achieve that state known as *bliss*?

Western medical traditions teach us that we can live our life however we want, without consequences. When we get sick, there will be a pill to "fix" us. High cholesterol? Again, a pill. Feeling a little down? Here's a bottle of anti-depressants. Are you obese? An appetite-suppressant will do the trick.

Even more so than the prescription-writing doctors and physicians, the all-powerful media takes it one step further by giving us the illusion that we can achieve better health by consuming the food industry's chemical concoctions, also known as processed foods. They want us to think we can eat whatever we want—as long as it's their version of reduced-fat, diet, sugar-free or fat-free. They tell us "calories in, calories out." That it doesn't really matter what we put into our mouths. And yet, years later, when our health inevitably fails us, the doctors will be waiting expectantly with a trove of pharmaceuticals and expensive surgeries to "fix" our problems for us.

Some try to stop time using pills, potions, procedures and other plastic surgery "cures" to look as young as possible. And if you can't afford plastic surgery, at least you can work your butt off in the gym to the point where you are emaciated enough to fit the media's picture of "beauty." Thin is in, but even if you're not, they tell us we can still be "fat and fit," even though movies and advertisements beg to differ. The women's magazines tell us to 'eat clean' and starve ourselves on 21-day juice fasts if we're feeling a little flabby, and yet the next pages advertise for fat-free yogurt, insulin-spiking vitamin water and highly processed sugary protein bars. The mixed messages are endless and overwhelming to the point where we feel powerless to stop them.

By relying on external sources for our health and well-being, we give away our personal power. We come to believe that we are not as knowledgeable or as able to care for ourselves as our physicians. We pass off the responsibility of self-care to someone else, because we have been taught that doctors are all-knowing and will always be able to "fix" us, no matter the concern.

Medical doctors do serve a very important function. There has been a good deal of research that has been incredibly valuable in regards to not only the care they provide, but also to the effectiveness of their treatment. But we can't underestimate the power of self-care—given by none other than, you guessed it: your pretty little self.

In determining the state of our health, we are far more powerful than we think. And to be truly healthy—and I don't mean being stick-thin or simply having acceptable numbers from your latest blood work—we must rely on ourselves to find our own ideal balance in these areas:

1. **Proper nutrition and exercise**
2. **Adequate rest**
3. **The ability to deal with stress**
4. **Meaningful relationships**
5. **A strong belief in a higher power**

We have to start somewhere, so let's get going!

Part 2

Your Body

It all starts with the body. Pain, relief, strength, weakness, fat, skinny, joy, grief—these all have physical and emotional connections. The power of your body to control, and even cause, happiness, pain, joy and sadness cannot be underestimated. Likewise, the link between our bodies and our brains is more significant and intense than ever imagined.

Deepak Chopra once said this about the mind-body connection: "Nothing holds more power over the body than the beliefs of the mind… In every moment, our cells are eavesdropping on our thoughts, feelings, and perceptions and being changed by them. This gives us an immense opportunity to use our mind and intentions to transform our biology."

I like to think of the body as a vessel—and it's the only one you'll ever get—so I empower my clients (and myself) to treat it in the best possible way.

The Body Eclectic

I always thought I was going to die from heart disease. My grandfather died of a heart attack at 35, and my grandmother at 60. My uncle had his first heart attack at age 34. What was surprising to everyone was when my mother died from something entirely different at the age of 54. Colon cancer.

Eventually, she starved to death. It was ironic because she had been obese her whole life. And yet when they operated for the third time, there was so much scar tissue left over that she couldn't eat or digest her food.

Cancer deaths are a close second to those from heart disease, affecting about 1/3 of the population. All of us have some cancer cells in our body, and yet my mother died from hers. It's easy to ask yourself "why" in a situation like that. But the *real* question becomes, how do some people keep cancer at bay, while others succumb?

Most people usually say, "Well, they caught it early."

The second response is often, "They had good surgeons."

But many of us neglect to consider the other important aspects of defending ourselves from cancer, illness and disease. The fact is, there is so much that can be done—outside of conventional Western medicine—to activate our body's natural defenses to prevent or avoid illness altogether.

But my mother wasn't interested in anything she considered "alternative." She treated her cancer the traditional way, through chemo and surgery. It may have treated the symptoms, and maybe even the disease, but it failed to take into account all the other aspects of the body that assist in disease prevention and healing: attitude, hope, state of mind, emotional health and more.

I watched her suffer in fear, doubt and uncertainty, and it pains me today to think of how a change in attitude and a few simple alternative remedies might have altered her course of treatment, even the course of her life.

My uncle, the one with heart disease, is a surgeon. When I showed him the research I had amassed to write this book, he was flabbergasted. He said he hadn't studied any of this in medical school. In fact, only 6 percent of medical doctors study something as basic as nutrition. Yet there is an endless amount of medical research available to support how nutrition can prevent and aid in the recovery from cancer and a host of other ailments.

Now more than ever, through understanding a host of foods, herbs and other natural remedies, we have the ability to not only prevent disease through our food choices, but to heal our bodies as well. With empowerment comes wellness, and hopefully what you learn in this section will awaken and enlighten you.

Nutrition

What do we know about nutrition? By that I mean, what do we *really* know? Many Americans are under the impression that they fully understand proper nutrition, and they work hard to secure it for themselves and their families. But how can we be so sure that what we're doing is right for us?

Most of us can afford to eat well, which to many people means plenty of animal products. Meat, cheese, milk, eggs and poultry are often the main ingredient in two or even three meals per day for most Americans. We know that plant foods, fruits and vegetables are good for us, but yet we rarely make them the main ingredients for our meals.

Modern wisdom claims that it is impossible to get enough protein or essential vitamins and minerals from a solely plant-based diet. However, when you separate the facts from the marketing claims, the actual research about what makes for proper nutrition is rather compelling.

In the West, our "Standard American Diet" (SAD) way of eating is costing us dearly. More food does not always mean better food. Sometimes it just means more food, and often of a lesser quality. One in three of us is obese, and this number is increasing almost annually. Yet heart disease, diabetes, multiple sclerosis, Alzheimer's and certain types of cancer are virtually non-existent in other parts of the world.

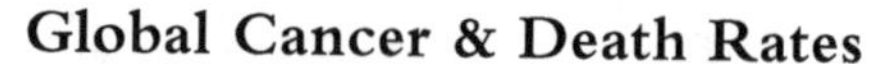

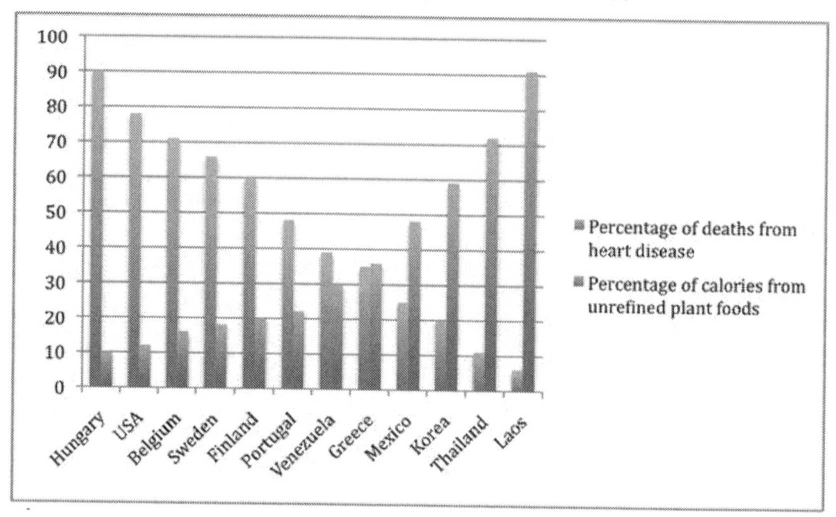

National Institutes of Health. Global cancer rates, cancer death rates among 50 countries, 1986-1999.

As you may see from the graph above, the countries that eat the most plants have the lowest rates of cancer and heart disease. Conversely, those that eat the least amount of plants (ie, the traditional Western diet) suffer from the highest rates of disease.

Diseases of Affluence

In Dr. Campbell's *The China Study*, I found the revelation that we can essentially "turn off" cancer cells using diet and lifestyle pretty exciting for two reasons:

1. Because we now realize that we have the ability to practice self-care. For decades, many of us felt powerless against our fates, figuring that if cancer, heart disease or Alzheimer's ran in the family, that we'd get it for sure. Now we know better. And that's pretty darn empowering!

2. Because nutrition is responsible for about 30 percent of cancers. That's the same percentage as smoking in relation to lung cancer! We all know that if we smoke, we have a greater chance of developing lung cancer, and yet are we equally aware that following a plant-based diet is so protective for overall health?

The Benefits of a Plant-Based Diet

Richard Béliveau, PhD in Biochemistry, is the director of the Molecular Medicine Laboratory and a researcher in the Department of Neurosurgery at Notre-Dame Hospital in Montreal. Dr. Béliveau has achieved astounding results in cancer treatment using food. He's also said, "With all I've learned over these years of research, if I were asked to design a diet today that promoted the development of cancer to the maximum, I couldn't improve on our present diet!"

And it's not just cancer. Dr. Caldwell Esselstyn of the Cleveland Clinic, which is considered to be one of the best heart centers in the world, has been working with heart patients for the past 20 years. He has been able to reverse their heart disease through diet. Dr. Caldwell calls heart disease a "toothless tiger that need not exist." I love it. No longer do we have to let disease and illness rule our lives with fear. We can regain control.

Power, Privilege and Politics

During World War II, meat and dairy products were rationed, and subsequently heart disease and cancer rates dropped significantly. As dietary patterns returned to normal shortly after the war, the rates of heart disease and cancer went back up to their pre-war status.

Mortality from Circulatory Disease in Norway in 1927-48

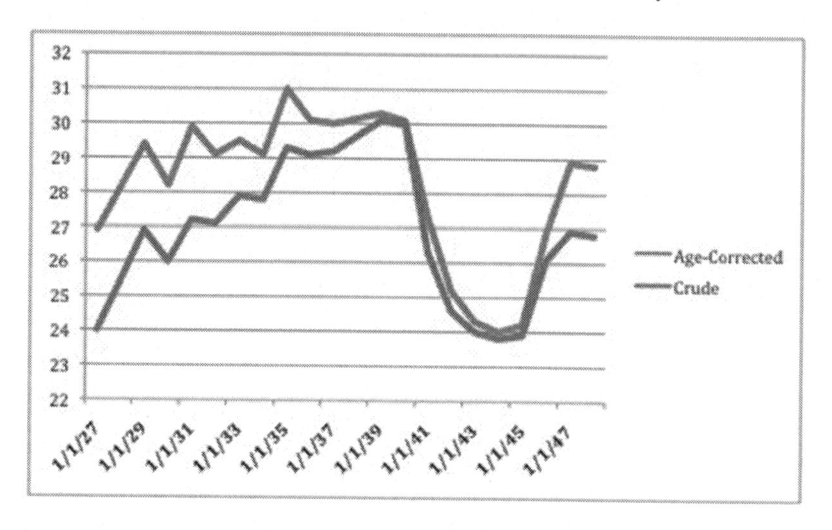

Vertical axis = death rate per 10,000 population.
Standard population = population of Norway in 1940.

Axel Strøm, R.Adelsten Jensen, M.D. Oslo, M.D. Oslo
MORTALITY FROM CIRCULATORY DISEASES IN NORWAY 1940-1945
The Lancet, Volume 257, Issue 6647, 20 January 1951, Pages 126-129.

This information was presented to a congressional committee that published a report called, "Dietary Goals for the United States," in which it recommended "lowering the consumption of meat and dairy products."

The person who had presided over the committee was Senator George McGovern. In a conversation that he had with French physician, author and neuroscientist David Servan-Schreiber, MD, PhD, Servan-Schreiber wrote, "McGovern was downcast and worried." He quoted McGovern as saying, "I've just made the biggest mistake of my political career."

Not surprisingly, three years later, the subsidies from the powerful cattle industry went to McGovern's political opponent, helping to end his career. Also not surprising was that these financial powerhouses, who funded many of the experts, were able to change the wording of the recommendations, leaving the public in a state of confusion as to what the proper nutritional course should be.

Today, the powerful forces of lobbyists for the meat and dairy industries combine with traditional media to shove the health benefits of beef, chicken, pork, eggs, milk and cheese down our throats at every possible opportunity—in print ads, newspaper stories, privately funded studies, vaguely worded reports and a variety of other measures that ensure that every time a story comes out touting the health benefits of a plant-based diet, two more follow cheering for the benefits of animal foods.

James W. Anderson, MD, a professor of Medicine and Clinical Nutrition, Emeritus, at the University of Kentucky, conducted trials with diabetic patients and was actually able to reverse type 2 diabetes using a high-fiber plant-based diet known as "The Simple Diet."

Two out of every three people in the US are overweight, and one in three is obese. Yet by following a high-fiber plant-based diet and engaging in regular exercise for three weeks, 4,500 patients from the Pritikin Longevity Center, a well-established wellness clinic that's been around since the 1960s, were able to lose on average 5.5 percent of their body weight. For a 130-pound woman, that would be a weight loss of more than 7 pounds.

According to Dr. Campbell, certain conditions like multiple sclerosis, kidney stones and Alzheimer's can sometimes be avoided with a plant-based diet. Sounds crazy, right? What you've just heard, in only a few pages, goes completely against everything you've probably been taught. But where are the headlines? Where are the news reports? I mean, if this were all true, we would know about it, right?

Think again. The sad fact is that traditional medicine is big money. Pharmaceutical companies, lobbyists, doctors, politicians, pharmacists and the like all benefit from the convenient "take a pill for your ill" mentality. Cheap disease prevention on the other hand, like using nutrition and exercise, would cost a lot of executives and industries a lot of money—much more than their money-hungry minds want to think about.

Imagine what might happen to the pharmaceutical industry if we began controlling and even preventing disease with the proper food. What if we tried drinking a glass of water or massaging our temples to relieve our headache before reaching for an aspirin? What if we tried avoiding trans-fatty fried foods in the first place rather than popping a heartburn pill? What about some chamomile tea and a relaxing bedtime routine before turning to a sleeping pill?

Our current way of thinking about nutrition, disease, food and health—as well as the connections between them—has been molded in such a way that the big pharmaceutical and medical industries will benefit most. But why?

Most people often believe that doctors have studied nutrition at some point during their schooling, and that they know all of this important information and are simply keeping it from us. That they could help us and fix our health if they merely spilled the beans and told us the truth. In reality, Western medicine is geared to treat disease only once it has already manifested, not to prevent it before it begins. And often their method of "fixing" the problem is with a potentially dangerous pill or expensive surgery—not using nutrition, lifestyle adjustments or another safer, less expensive way.

Medical schools often view nutrition as a "soft skill," a luxury instead of a necessity. They use surgery and drugs and are excellent at keeping abreast of scientific advances, but there is little room in the curriculum for nutritional studies of a preventative nature.

When you think about it, there is little benefit to the medical establishments and drug companies, from a strictly financial standpoint, to teach the benefits of nutrition. When you consider that it costs about $500 million to a billion dollars to conduct experiments—including those involving nutrition—on humans, it's no wonder that they find it too much of a bother to invest more time and money in studying nutrition's effects on our health and well-being.

Then again, what should be more precious to humans than preserving human life? Life that is healthy, happy, long and joyful? To me, there can be no price tag too high for that! But from their perspective, an investment is justified when a minor anticancer medicine can bring in a billion dollars a year to the company that holds the patent. On the other hand, who stands to benefit from eating more broccoli?

FAQs About Plant-Based Diets:

Ok, maybe this all sounds interesting, but it's pretty new stuff. I know. It's a lot to take in! You probably have questions about eating a plant-based diet, so below I've included some science-based answers to the most common questions I'm asked:

- **Won't going without meat make me feel weak, hungry and irritable?** Actually, the American Public Health Association found that going vegetarian *improves* mood for some people. (**Source**: *December 2009 American Public Health Association*)
- **Don't I need it to be strong and healthy?** People who consumed the least amount of red and processed meat products had reduced risk for heart disease, diabetes and colorectal cancer, compared with those who consumed the most, according to a 2012 study. (**Source**: *2012 British Medical Journal Open*)
- **Don't I need dairy products for healthy bones?** No. In fact, animal protein has been shown to be associated with a *decrease* in bone health, according to a 2010 study. (**Source**: *March 2010 British Journal of Nutrition)*
- **I thought carbs were fattening, shouldn't I be avoiding them?** According to a recent study, a low-carbohydrate, high-protein diet greatly boosts the risk of heart disease. (**Source**: *2012 British Medical Journal*)

- **But if I've been eating meat all my life, aren't my arteries already shot?** A healthy vegetarian diet along with the right lifestyle choices, including exercise and stress management, can rejuvenate coronary arteries. (**Source**: *February 2010 American Journal of Cardiology*)
- **Can eating more fruits and vegetables help prevent any types of cancer?** Eating more fruits and vegetables can increase survival rates in women with ovarian cancer. Authors of a 2010 study concluded that a plant-based diet is not only good for prevention but also for improving and increasing survival time. (**Source**: *March 2010 Journal of American Dietetic Association*)
- **What about breast cancer?** Based on 34,000 women in the Singapore Chinese Health study, eating more fruits and vegetables reduced the risk of breast cancer. (**Source**: *March 2010 American Journal of Clinical Nutrition*)
- **What other health benefits can you point to that are directly related to switching to a plant-based diet?** Vegetarians often have lower: blood pressure, waist circumference, body mass index, blood sugar and triglycerides, compared with non-vegetarians. (**Source**: *April 2011 Diabetes Care*)
- **What if I'm a guy? Is this a realistic lifestyle for me?** It's not only realistic, it can change your life. Vegetarian men weigh less and have less cardiovascular disease risk compared with non-vegetarians. (**Source**: *September 2011 Nutrition and Metabolism*)
- **How bad can red meat really be?** Eating large amounts of red meat was shown to increase the risk of kidney cancer by 19 percent, compared to those who ate the least amount. The intake of well-done grilled and barbequed meat was also linked to an increased kidney cancer risk. (**Source**: *January 2012 American Journal of Clinical Nutrition*)

- **Are whole grains preventative against any types of cancer?** Whole grains have been shown to reduce the risk of colorectal cancer. (**Source**: *February 2012 British Medical Journal*)
- **What about heart disease?** A low-carbohydrate, high-protein diet has been shown to boost the risk of heart disease. (**Source**: *July 2012 British Medical Journal*)
- **Will switching to a plant-based diet reduce my risk of stroke?** If done correctly, yes, as red and processed meats have been linked with an increase in stroke risk. (**Source**: *August 2012, the American Heart Association*)
- **Where will I get my protein?** Don't worry, I gotcha covered! The chart below shows a variety of delicious ways you can get protein while enjoying a plant-based diet:

Nuts/Seeds (4 Tbsp, or 1/4 cup)	**Protein (g)**
Chia Seeds	12
Hemp Seeds	10
Flax Seeds	8
Sunflower Seeds	8
Salbas	7.4
Almonds	7
Pumpkin Seeds	7
Sesame Seeds	7
Pistachios	6
Walnuts	5
Brazil Nuts	5
Hazelnuts	5
Pine Nuts	4
Cashews	4

Beans (1 cup cooked)	**Protein (g)**
Lentils	18
Adzukis	17
Cannellinis (white beans)	17

Cranberry Beans	17
Navy Beans	16
Split Peas	16
Anasazi Beans	15
Black Beans	15
Garbanzos (Chickpeas)	15
Kidney Beans	15
Great Northern Beans	15
Lima Beans	15
Pink Beans	15
Black-Eyed Peas	14
Mung Beans	14
Pinto Beans	14
Green Peas	9

Grains (1 cup cooked)	**Protein (g)**
Triticale	25
Millet	8.4
Amaranth	7
Oat, bran	7
Wild Rice	7
Rye Berries	7
Whole Wheat Couscous	6
Bulgar Wheat	6
Buckwheat	6
Teff	6
Oat Groats	6
Barley	5
Quinoa	5
Brown Rice	5
Spelt	5

Vegetables (cooked)	**Protein (g)**
Corn (1 large cob)	5

Potato (with skin)	5
Mushroom, Oyster (1 cup)	5
Collard Greens (1 cup)	4
Peas (1/2 cup)	4
Artichoke (medium)	4
Broccoli (1 cup)	4
Brussels Sprouts (1 cup)	4
Mushroom, Shiitake (1 cup)	3.5
Fennel (1 medium bulb)	3
Swiss Chard (1 cup)	3
Kale (1 cup)	2.5
Asparagus (5 spears)	2
String Beans (1 cup)	2
Beets (1 cup)	2
Sweet Potato (1 cup)	3
Cabbage	2
Carrot (1 cup)	2
Cauliflower (1 cup)	2
Rutabaga	2
Squash	2
Celery (1 cup)	1
Spinach (1 cup)	1
Bell Pepper (1 cup)	1
Cucumber (1 cup)	1
Eggplant (1 cup)	1
Leek (1 cup)	1
Okra (1/2 cup)	1
Onion (1/2 cup)	1

Now compare those options to a 100-gram serving of steak, which contains 17 grams of protein. And take a peek at the chart below for all the other junk you'll be skipping out on by enjoying plant-based sources of protein instead of those from animals:

Nutrient Composition of Plant and Animal-Based Foods (per 500 calories of energy)

Nutrient	Plant-Based Foods*	Animal-Based Foods**
Cholesterol (mg)	---	137
Fat (g)	4	36
Protein (g)	33	34
Beta-Carotene (mcg)	29,919	17
Dietary Fiber (g)	31	---
Vitamin C (mg)	293	4
Folate (mcg)	1168	19
Vitamin E (mg_ATE)	11	0.5
Iron (mg)	20	2
Magnesium (mg)	548	51
Calcium (mg)	545	252

Holden, J.M., Eldridge, A.L., Beecher, G.R., Buzzard, I.M., Bhagwat, S.A., Davis, C.S., Douglass, Larry, W., Gebhardt, S.E., Haytowitz, D.B., and Schakel, S. 1999. "Carotenoid Content of U.S. Foods: An Update of the Database." *J. Food Comp. Anal.* 12:169-196.

***Plant-Based Food Sources**: Raw spinach; raw Russet potatoes (skin included); large mature raw lima beans; raw green peas; and raw ripe red tomatoes.

****Animal-Based Food Sources**: Equal parts raw ground beef (80% lean meat, 20% fat); raw broiler/fryer chicken (meat and skin); whole milk (dried); and raw ground pork.

Fear is On the Menu

Our dietary habits are part of our traditions. We're raised to have certain beliefs and customs, as were our parents and their parents before them. It's amazing how closely our modern diets are tied to those our parents and grandparents ate decades earlier, before most of the discoveries about the dangers of meat, dairy, fat, sugar and cholesterol.

We were taught that breakfast was either cold—cereal, milk and juice—or hot, with eggs, bacon or sausage, grits or potatoes and toast with butter and jam. Lunch was a sandwich and chips, or burgers and fries, or some kind of meat and side dish. Dinner was definitely meat, possibly with a small salad and side dishes consisting of potatoes or some other starch.

We learn these habits early on in life, just as our parents did before them. The problem is, childhood habits can be particularly hard to break, and even once broken still continue to haunt us.

My grandmother was in Hawaii when she had her first heart attack, and my mother and I flew to the hospital to see her. She received nutritional counseling and was told not to eat processed meats. But my grandmother grew up eating salami and absolutely loved the stuff. She actually started to cry when she was told she would have to give it up; she couldn't bear the idea of giving up her favorite food.

And actually, she never *was* able to get used to the idea. She snuck salami into her room at every chance! My grandma also never quite started the diet that the nutritional counselor had recommended. She passed away six months later.

We can all attest to how difficult it can be to break a habit. Most doctors who know about the advantages of plant-based foods don't even approach the subject with their patients, as they believe that they simply won't want to make a change. They think, *why bother*? Or worse, they fear they will be perceived as a quack. In reality, research shows that most people who are educated are more prepared to make more radical changes, even if they've created lifelong habits that they know will be hard to break.

When informed of a health benefit or made aware of a new study or report, most people come equipped with the tools to make rational, informed decisions and will make the dietary shift as well as the lifestyle shifts that are needed to take advantage of the new habit.

Imagine not telling someone an important piece of information simply because you *assume* they won't be interested or willing to make changes—which may not be the case at all! Information is power, and not empowering patients is doing them a disservice. Giving people the information and then supporting the process, on the other hand, is a step toward positive change.

Battling Our Food Addictions

We are literally addicted to fat, salt and sugar. Research has shown that these substances cause the same feelings of physical dependence as heroin or cocaine. Yikes! In experiments conducted at Princeton University, when sugar was discontinued on test subjects, the rats began to exhibit signs of withdrawal, including "the shakes."

This physical dependency could account for why Americans are swallowing 22 teaspoons of sugar every day, which comes out to roughly 150 pounds a year per person. Not per household, not per family, not per square mile—per person!

Assuming you don't eat your sugar straight out of the bag, you might not believe the statistic above. But that's just it: most of the sugar we consume is conveniently "hidden" in all sorts of food and drinks—oftentimes in items that we wouldn't even think would have added sugar. Your sandwich may not taste so sweet, but more than likely, that bread is loaded up with added sugar!

Other common sources for hidden sugars include condiments like ketchup and barbecue sauce, cereals, muffins, frozen meals, granola bars and protein bars—even the "healthy" ones—fruit juices, and of course soft drinks and candy. Even bottled tea! Tea's supposed to be healthy, though, right? Only if you make it yourself. Most store-bought bottled and canned teas are loaded with sweeteners. How else will they get you to come back for more?

While sugar might not seem so bad, take a look at what these substances do to our body, and then see how you feel:

- **Cancer feeds on sugar:** When we consume sugar, the body releases a dose of insulin as well as insulin-like growth factor (IGF), which nourishes cancer cells, makes cancer tissue grow faster and promotes inflammation. In Dr. Servan-Schreiber's book, *Anticancer: A New Way of Life*, he says, "Today we know that the peaks of insulin growth and the secretion of IGF directly stimulates not only the growth of cancer cells but also their capacity to invade their neighboring tissue." Studies have also shown that eating a diet higher in high-glycemic foods is associated with cancer of the colon, prostate, pancreas and ovaries.

  High-glycemic carbohydrates are also known as simple carbs, or simple sugars. A bag of potato chips, a glass of fruit juice or a candy bar would all qualify. Then there are the low-glycemic carbs, also known as complex carbs, which include most vegetables, unprocessed whole grains, beans and legumes.

  Even certain fruits and vegetables can be high-glycemic, depending on how you eat them. For example, a glass of orange juice is high on the glycemic index because it only contains the sugars of the fruit; the fiber has been removed in the refining process. A whole orange, on the other hand, is lower on the glycemic index because the fibrous pulp takes longer to break down in the body for energy, slowing down the absorption of sugars and balancing blood sugar levels more so than an insulin-spiking glass of sugar water—orange juice, soda or otherwise.

  The glycemic index concept can be tricky to grasp at first, but to keep it simple, just remember that foods eaten in their whole, unprocessed form (ie, a whole orange) are more likely to be low-glycemic and good for you, whereas processed foods (ie, store-bought processed orange juice) are much more likely to be high-glycemic, resulting in imbalanced blood sugar levels and unstable energy levels.

So while a bag of potato chips is high-glycemic, a whole baked potato is less so. A rice cake will be higher on the glycemic index than unprocessed whole grain brown rice, and an apple is more balancing for blood sugar levels than a container of applesauce or a glass of apple juice. Bottom line: stay as close to the natural, unprocessed form as possible! This is a good rule of thumb for healthy eating in general, and it's an easy one to remember. Maybe not quite as easy to practice, but with time it will become second nature. Be patient with yourself and keep at it—the benefits will be worth it.

- **Heart Disease:** A study published by the *Journal of the American Medical Association* found that people who got at least 1/4 of their daily calories from added sugars of any kind were more than three times as likely to have low levels of the "good" cholesterol in their bloodstream.

Overcoming an addiction or dependence on sugar takes time. Dr. Douglas Lisle, who has spent the last two decades researching and studying this evolutionary syndrome, says that we all have what he calls "The Motivational Triad," which leads us to three distinct motivations:

1. **The pursuit of pleasure**
2. **The avoidance of pain**
3. **The conservation of energy**

Unfortunately, these same basic instincts that once successfully ensured our survival and reproduction no longer serve us well in modern times—where food is around every corner and survival is a matter of avoiding temptation rather than averting a threat of real danger.

Dr. Lisle explains that the human body has been hardwired to choose the most calorically dense foods. Our survival mechanism required us to value a mango over lettuce in order to pack on pounds for when food grew scarce. This served us well when we were scavenging and food was hard to find. Today, however, food is anything but scarce.

On top of that, the food-like concoctions of modern time are often designed to encourage us to eat as much as possible. From flavored waters to sugary protein bars, chemical additives, aspartame-ridden diet drinks and sugarless chewing gums, reduced-fat and fat-free to sugar free, foods are chemically altered to tease and hook our taste buds from the very first bite. Former Food and Drug Administration commissioner Dr. David Kessler once said, "We're living in a food carnival, these flavors are so stimulating they are hijacking our brains."

It's not surprising that we crave unhealthy foods when we are being purposefully manipulated to eat them. The precise combinations of chemicals, additives and flavorings drive us back to the trough again and again. If this sounds hard to believe, check out the *60 Minutes* episode called "The Flavorists: Tweaking tastes and creating cravings." After all, the more products food companies sell, the more money they make. But who gets rich selling Brussels sprouts?

The good news is, we *can* break this tricky cycle of food addiction.

Are You Ready for a Transformation?

Our habits are in a perpetual loop. In yoga, we call it the "Karmic loop." It works like this: you have a memory of something, which triggers a desire that leads you to take action. In Charles Duhigg's book, *The Power of Habit,* he explains it more scientifically: Wolfram Schultz, a professor of neuroscience at the University of Cambridge, conducted an experiment on monkeys where he gave them juice if they touched a lever when a shape appeared. They were conditioned to understand that the shapes were a cue for a routine (touch the lever) that resulted in a reward (juice).

From a neurological perspective, the behavior became an ingrained habit. What interested Schultz the most is that after repeated practice, the monkeys started craving the juice. When the juice was withheld, the monkeys became angry or depressed. This helps to explain why our habits become so powerful: they create neurological cravings.

Most of the time we are not even aware that these habits exist. We receive a cue—or, in yogic terms, a memory—which lead to a craving or desire. This desire then motivates us to take action (or, *Karma*). So, how do we break the habit cycle? By creating *new* habits.

First, we have to become conscious of what is driving the habit. That's where meditation and journaling come in. Meditation allows you to witness your patterns of behavior without reacting. And journaling lets you see your patterns and habits right there on the page in front of you. Becoming aware of our habits, patterns and behaviors is always the first step in moving towards positive change.

I believe that if we simply see the patterns for what they are—ie, eating out of boredom vs. actual hunger, we can begin to change our habits for the better. For example, do you reach for food when you're stressed? Are you always running out the door with no time to sit down to a decent meal, so you grab something pre-packed, quick, convenient and less than healthy? Do you eat when you're bored, lonely or sad? Do you take coffee breaks just to socialize with your coworkers and end up eating too many donuts without even thinking about it? Each time you notice the behavior, you can come up with an alternative solution. For instance, you can start to:

- **Plan your meals ahead of time to avoid impulse and temptation**
- **Have pre-packed healthy snacks ready to "grab and go"**
- **Keep track of what you eat and when**
- **Pay attention to when you eat and why**

Once you've come up with a list of realistic alternatives, you can start to actively replace your old habits with new ones.

So if you know you tend to eat when you're feeling bored or lonely, next time try calling a friend, check out Facebook or share a new plant-based food recipe online or with a friend. If you eat out of habit, simply because it's mealtime and you're "supposed to," try delaying lunch by half an hour and see if you're any more or less hungry.

After some successful changes in behavior, reward yourself—whether it's big or small. You deserve it! Positive reinforcement can make all the difference, especially in the beginning, as changing a habit or setting a new one takes 3 weeks. Those 21 days can be difficult if you're dealing with re-setting long-held behaviors, so make sure to thank yourself for all the hard work. And remember, you're worth the struggle and hard work! So keep at it.

If your goal is to fit into that bathing suit, keep a picture of it in plain view. Tape it to your fridge. Or if you're dieting to get healthy, reward yourself along the way. And just a thought: a reward doesn't have to involve food! So many of us have been conditioned to think of a 'treat' as something we put in our mouths, whether it's downing a pint of Ben & Jerry's or giving in to your late-night chocolate chip cookie cravings.

Try non-junk-food rewards instead: the good feelings will last much longer, plus you don't have to worry about any risk of post-binge guilt or stomachache. Have a manicure. Get a massage. Go to the farmer's market and buy that bouquet of bright, cheery flowers you've been eyeing, or splurge on those organic raspberries you keep passing up for the less expensive items. Treat yourself *without* junk foods so that you can keep your goals aligned with real life perspective and priorities.

The fact is, breaking dysfunctional food habits is transformational. You are literally changing one of the most fundamental habits of your life. Food is used for celebrations and has many cultural and even religious associations. You are creating new patterns, and like anything else, they will evolve over time.

For example, if when you think of a birthday party the image of birthday cake or treats floods your mind, it will take time for you to develop new associations every time a celebration comes around. A beautiful watermelon cut into smiley faces, along with strawberries and banana slices dipped in organic dark chocolate are other alternatives that are just as pleasing to the taste buds, and even more pleasing to the body and mind.

And what about settling into your favorite seat in your favorite movie theater, about to watch the summer's most anticipated blockbuster without a big bag of buttery, salted popcorn? Well, unbuttered popcorn sprinkled with nutritional yeast makes a tasty, healthy alternative. As you can see, food cues affect us both physically and mentally, and it will take effort, patience and perseverance to break lifelong habits. If you slip up, be kind to yourself. None of us is perfect! If you give into temptation, don't tell yourself it's a lost cause and throw in the towel. For every step forward, there may be two steps back, and that's OK. Just get right back on track and move forward.

As with anything new, recognize that there will be times when you not only miss the food but also the nostalgia of the association, like with birthday cakes and movie popcorn. It can be a lot like quitting smoking or drinking incessantly. First you become educated, and then you make the decision to change your habit. Then you struggle with the new behavior, and finally you begin to adapt and change.

Today we look back at smoking on airplanes with disbelief, yet not that long ago, it was considered normal. What will our children and their children look back on in horror that we once considered normal? Candy bars, aspartame-ridden diet sodas and fast food drive-thrus? One can only hope!

So let's take a step back and consider your personal food transformation. Change will occur whether you are willing to let it happen or not, but whether or not you accept it and go with the flow will determine your experience of the situation.

The more you struggle to keep things the same, the more difficulty you will probably have adopting change. What I found helpful in adapting to new behaviors was finding the benefits of the change and focusing on those.

For example, if you're changing your dietary patterns, it may help to focus on all the new flavors and tastes you'll get to experience, many for the first time. Imagine trying to vary your menu with new styles of cooking exotic fruits and satisfying, healthy vegetables. Your body will benefit from these changes, which will positively reinforce your behavior—if you let it. You may find new favorite restaurants, which will expand your community and allow you to meet new people. Imagine trying Indian food for the first time, or Thai, or sushi!

Think of yourself as being in a food rut that will be broken wide open to explore new tastes, new health benefits and fun new combinations. Change is exciting. Change provides opportunity. Change is *good*. Try your best to be open to these opportunities. Only then will you receive the full benefits.

Try it Now

To round out our section on the body, try this simple exercise in your notebook:

- **List a few fun new experiences you want to have as a result of your new food choices and habits.**
- **List out some ways that you think practicing change will be good for you.**
- **Write down why you think food may be a good way to practice accepting and embracing change.**

What else do you have to say about this whole process? Let it all out on paper! The simple act of writing something down—whether using pen and paper, your computer or even the corner of a paper napkin—can be surprisingly therapeutic. If it makes you feel more comfortable, rip up the pages when you're done, this way you can vent without the fear of anyone seeing what you've written.

Taking Your Health Back: *The Plant-Based Challenge*

As you begin the gradual shift from a Western diet to whole plant-based foods, try to think of it this way: a new habit may be hard to swallow at first, but if you give it enough time, you will get used to it and even end up enjoying it.

In an attempt to make the process a little easier to start, I've listed the steps you'll want to take in order to support your dietary process:

- **Get a notebook and a calendar.**
- **Write a list of all the things that you want from your healthy lifestyle.** It can be anything, from fitting into a favorite dress or reversing type 2 diabetes.
- **To prepare yourself for the ups and downs, make a list of all the things that could stand in your way**. For example:
  - Not having enough time to cook
  - Getting bored of eating the same foods
  - The spouse and/or kids being resistant or unsupportive
  - Whatever else you feel could make this difficult for you
- **Now, think about some possible solutions to the obstacles you just listed**. So if you think time will be an issue, could you prepare food for the week on a weekend afternoon or evening when you have more time? Or if boredom may be an issue, think of ways you could spice up the selection or preparation of vegetables for you and your family.
- **Mark a date on the calendar that you will start your commitment.**
- **On that starting date, write down your starting weight, or take note of it mentally**.

- **Look at all the commitments you have over the next few weeks.**
  Are there any you could put off until you get adjusted to this new way of living? All those people that need you also want you healthy and strong. You will do them no good if you don't take care of yourself first. It's kind of like that airplane safety announcement when they tell you to first put on your own mask before helping others.
- **Before you begin, realize and try to accept that mistakes will happen**. Also realize that when they do, you are only one meal away from getting right back on track.

Part 3

Your Mind

Whenever your brain perceives something as a threat, from a minor stressor to a seriously dangerous situation, your body will go through the same physiological process, preparing you for attack, or "flight."

Let's say your boss walks over to your desk and says that she wants to meet with you tomorrow to discuss some recent issues with your work. Or let's say you were driving a bit too high over the speed limit, and all of a sudden you hear police sirens coming from somewhere behind you. And then there are the obviously stressful events, like you're walking home alone at night and someone starts following close behind you.

Those events all trigger the same sequence of physiological responses in the body: the heart beats faster, blood pressure rises, sweating increases, the adrenal glands pump out more adrenaline and cortisol, the pancreas releases glucagon and increases blood glucose levels, the immune system is suppressed, less healing and rejuvenating hormones are released, and blood flow moves away from the digestive organs and towards the muscles, so you can forget about effectively breaking down the nutrients in that lunch you just had. No matter how seemingly minor the event may seem to your conscious rational mind, if your brain perceives it as any sort of threat, the body will react.

Your Brain On Stress: *Fight or Flight (Or… Eat!)*

As you may already know, our minds are incredibly powerful. They are also completely connected with our bodies. Your body is always listening carefully and responding accordingly to your thoughts and feelings while you're awake—even if you can't feel it.

One example of this can be seen in the story of a man named Tom Boyle, Jr. After eating dinner one evening, he saw a young boy caught under a Camaro and sprung into action. With his heart pumping and the adrenaline surging through his body, he was somehow able to lift the car off the trampled boy. His mind, recognizing danger and filling his body with adrenaline and other powerful chemicals and hormones, allowed his body to respond in a way that it might not have been able to in its "resting" state, or without his mind responding to the implied danger of a young boy's impending death.

You might think that you lead a normal sedentary life, but the fact is that our minds and bodies are always on high alert for even the slightest hint of danger or stress—even if it's only in our head. By some estimates, Americans have thirty to forty fight-or-flight episodes per day. It doesn't take a hungry saber tooth tiger clawing at the door or a criminal ready to mug you in some dark back alley to set our minds on high alert and flood our bodies with stress hormones.

Let's say you're driving in traffic and someone cuts you off. You have to swerve or brake quickly to avoid hitting them, most likely resulting in a brief fight-or-flight response. Or let's say your boss walks over to your desk and tells you that he or she wants you to present your latest research to the company at the next town hall meeting (and you HATE speaking in public). Your brain and body may start to panic.

Imagine what is happening to your body during each one of these episodes. The first reaction is physical stress: the changes your body goes through under stress, fight or flight. Next, after you're assured that there is no mugger or physical danger present, the emotional stress occurs—the flutter in your stomach, the stress headache. These are all very real emotional outcomes of the fight-or-flight response, which has both a physical and emotional undercurrent. Fortunately, there is an antidote to all this: meditation, which we'll get to in a bit.

One side effect from all of these fight-or-flight episodes is our natural tendency for "stress eating." In an article by *Harvard Health* from February 2012, the authors explain how stress unleashes cortisol, a hormone that may cause us to overeat. So it goes a little like this: you feel stress, and then drained after the release of hormones that stress triggers and to compensate for those feelings, you rush to your favorite sugary, high-fat, carb-heavy "comfort" food to restore the delicate balance to your system. The more stress you feel, the more common this comfort food habit becomes, and inevitably the more weight you gain.

Researchers have linked weight gain to stress, and this spells bad news for many of us, as one out of every four Americans rate their stress level as 8 or more on a 10-point scale!

Stress also seems to affect food preferences. Numerous studies have shown that physical or emotional distress increases the intake of food that is high in fat, sugar or both. High cortisol levels, in combination with high insulin levels, may be responsible. Other research suggests that ghrelin, a "hunger hormone," may play a role.

Once ingested, fatty and sugary foods seem to have a feedback effect that inhibits activity in the parts of the brain that produce and process stress and related emotions. These really are "comfort" foods in that they seem to counteract stress—and this may contribute to people's stress-induced craving for comfort foods.

The cycle is a lot like the drinking seawater. Sure, your thirst may be quenched momentarily, but the aftereffect in your body will only force you to crave more and more water in an unquenchable feedback loop. Likewise, the more you seek comfort from these fatty, salty and calorie-laden foods, the more they will force you to come back for more.

Of course, overeating isn't the only stress-related behavior that can pack on the pounds. Stressed people also lose sleep, exercise less and drink more alcohol, all of which can contribute to excess weight. So let's get our stress levels under control to curb all of that. How? I'm glad you asked! Let me introduce you to meditation, one of my dearest friends.

Meditation: *The (Natural) Antidote to Stress*

So what can we do about all this stress? It's not like we can just quit our jobs or ship the kids off to camp for the summer if it's too much to handle. Instead, I offer you one simple word: *meditation.* As we meditate—even as beginners—our heart rate and breathing slow, and we naturally lower our blood pressure.

Meditation is the natural antidote to stress because almost everything about it is the opposite of stress. Instead of releasing cortisol, like our bodies do when stressed, meditation releases those so-called "feel good" hormones like serotonin and oxytocin. Yep, that's the same wonderful chemical that floods the body after cuddling and orgasm. And serotonin's importance can't be overstated—it's the body's natural anti-depressant.

The best part is, this harmonious stress-antidote effect is not only present while we meditate. In a study led by Harvard-affiliated neuroscientist Sara Lazar, she was able to show that meditation actually *changes your brain.* So we feel the positive effects even after the meditation session is over.

For eight weeks, Lazar took MRIs of peoples' brains before and after they meditated. She found that meditation changed the grey matter of the subjects' brains. The hippocampus, that part of the brain that controls memory, sense of self, compassion and empathy, actually grew, while the amygdala, the part of the brain responsible for anxiety and stress, shrank.

Maybe you've heard Carl Shatz's expression, "Neurons that fire together wire together." So not only are we able to reduce our stress when we meditate, but we are able to actually change our habits and our brain—for good.

As we meditate, we are able to develop the role of the "witnessing observer." We place our focus on our breath or mantra, and as our attention wanders away, we train ourselves to bring it back. Each time we strengthen the ability to notice our repetitive thoughts or feelings, we learn to take a step back and observe and self-monitor what's going on inside our head. We can then recognize the physical and emotional triggers and teach ourselves new habits to replace the old.

In her book *Healing Mind, Healthy Woman*, Alice Domar, PhD, writes, "Fat is a mind body issue, food is a health issue… One-dimensional approaches will not resolve eating disorders because their causes run deep."

These deeper causes are often the reason why quick fixes, fad diets or one-dimensional diets don't work. They might put a bandage on the problem for a few weeks as some initial weight is lost, but unless a program goes deeper to touch root causes and change long-established habits, it is unfortunately doomed to fail, and the weight will likely return sooner or later.

Unlike pop culture self-help or spot-reducing one's abs or thighs, the holistic practice of mind-body medicine instead addresses root causes, like anxiety, the feeling of not being in control, internalized negative beliefs about beauty and success, unhealthy expectations, a sense of emptiness and damaged self worth. That goes a *little* deeper than a 20-minute ab routine.

Our deeply rooted (but changeable) habitual behavior is one reason why we continue to make poor food choices, despite knowing that it's better for us to eat more fruits and veggies.

How Do You Explain Your Life?

According to yogic tradition, our psyches are made up of three distinct parts:

1. **Our mind**
2. **Our intellect**
3. **Our ego**

Similarly, these three aspects of our personality also make up our *explanatory style*, or how we see the world. The first part, our mind, is like a video camera. It takes in and records all the sights and sounds. Then, our intellect "edits" our film, deciding what parts of the recording we like, and how we feel about it. Our intellect makes up our continuously running internal dialogue, or our "story." It decides what ends up on the cutting room floor and what makes it into the film that makes up our internal life. Then there's the ego, which puts its own spin on all this.

Let's look at an example of how this process works. So the video camera (our mind) sees water falling from the sky. Our editor (our intellect) decides this is bad, and then our ego makes the story all about us. Suddenly, our internal dialogue sounds a lot like, "My day is ruined, I hate rain. It's going to smudge my makeup and make me late for work. Why does this always happen to me?"

Ultimately, our ego is like the diva of our movie. Notice how our diva just had to steal the show. I'm pretty sure that rain had nothing to do with us, but notice how it came back to us anyways. The stories that we tell ourselves are really important—so important that they affect our health, or even the success or failure of our diets.

Martin Seligman, author of *Learned Optimism: How to Change Your Mind and Your Life*, studied people's explanatory styles (their worldview) and found that people who had negative styles actually got sicker. In fact, of thirty-four women that were interviewed for a National Cancer Institute study, those who where optimistic lived longer.

Martin Seligman: *Habitual Behavior and Learned Optimism*

Our habits don't just affect our lives, they *define* them. Martin Seligman wrote, "Depression results from lifelong habits of conscious thought. If we can change these habits of thought, we will cure depression."

Habitual thought can find you reaching for a sweet snack even when you're not hungry, just because it's the time of day that you always reach for a snack, or because you're stressed and you need your "comfort" food.

In a nutshell, Seligman's saying that the way we explain things to ourselves affects whether we feel *in* control of our lives or whether we experience what he calls "learned helplessness," a habitual sense that nothing we do will ever matter anyway, so why bother? But Seligman says that we can learn optimism, that we can create positive mental habits, and what's more, that a pattern of learned helplessness affects our health, making our immune system more passive. The immune system is involved in a host of important functions throughout the body, so this is kind of a big deal!

Optimists resist helplessness. In seeing the brighter side of any situation, they can better process setbacks, dark clouds and even sickness by dealing with it in a more healthful manner.

So, what about you? Have you learned helplessness as a habit, or can you learn optimism to help change your habits? See if either of these styles sounds more like you:

> *You have been on a diet for the past few weeks. You are out for drinks with friends and you eat a couple of the nachos several of your friends ordered. Feeling guilty about the slight digression, you immediately think to yourself:*

"I'm such a pig! I can't even control myself! What's the point? I might as well go home and finish the cake in the freezer. . ."

OR:

"No problem, tomorrow's another day. I can get right back on track and make this diet work. What's a few nachos anyways?"

If you tend to think, "What's the point?," then you are displaying signs of learned helplessness. If you think, "Okay, so I messed up, I can hop right back on the horse," you are displaying optimism, learned or otherwise.

Let's go back to how the three parts of your psyche—your mind, your intellect and your ego—make up what we call your explanatory style. If you want to "learn optimism," you need to readjust how you explain the events of your life.

If, for instance, you blow your diet, you need to retrain your mind, your intellect *and* your ego to think positive thoughts, to craft a more positive, actionable outlook on life so that all is not lost. Let's say your internal video recorder (your mind) finds you pigging out on a Saturday night. Okay, fine, a few donuts and a pint of ice cream later, you're feeling less than positive about your outlook.

Now it's time for your editor (your intellect) to get to work. It's important to leave the "bad" stuff on the cutting room floor and instead focus on what you *can* do to recover your positive mental attitude. Of this event, what can you salvage? For instance, maybe you didn't eat all six of the donuts you bought. Or maybe you tossed out half of that pint of ice cream so at least you wouldn't feel full to bursting. Those positive points should all be part of your explanation for this part of the story.

Finally, your inner diva, your ego, needs to find something to focus on next. How to recover? Tell yourself that tomorrow morning you'll get up and burn those calories off. Picture yourself doing it. Lay your exercise clothes out, set your alarm and do something positive to recover from the not-so-good, and your outlook will start to learn to focus on the positive instead of the negative.

This next section continues this focus and will help you "retrain" your internal dialogue to support a more optimistic explanatory style AND worldview.

Digging Yourself Out

So, how do you change your self-dialogue? Well, first you have to be conscious of what it is. During my own personal tragedy, I was so wrapped up in my survival story ("How can I support my family? I'm all alone! Everybody I love dies. I'm no good.") that I couldn't see my self-dialogue for what it was: *destructive.*

When you stop to meditate, you can more clearly notice which stories, patterns and internal dialogues you are repeating. For me, I was able to change the negative "How will I support my family? How dare they throw me out?" message to something more positive, like, "Wow, what an opportunity! Now I get to shine on my own! In a family business I never got to feel significant. Now I will get to show what I can do." This was a major breakthrough. These positive messages to myself allowed me to move forward in a more optimistic way.

Through meditation and powerful, positive focus, my "My mother died, poor me" message changed to, "She is always with me. Let me internalize her values and hopes and dreams and make her proud." In fact, my turnaround was so powerful that part of the reason I am writing this book is to make her death into something meaningful.

My internal talk changed from, "I'm no good. I'm such a failure, I can't believe I'm divorced," to, "Let me learn and grow from all this." We all have parts of ourselves that need improvement. The first step is being aware of those parts so that we can change them and move forward in a more positive and constructive way. Instead of scolding myself for all the ways I thought I'd failed, I changed my perspective so that I could use the failed marriage as an opportunity to better understand myself and move forward a stronger person.

This transformation from the negative to the positive didn't happen overnight, of course, so don't expect too much from yourself all at once. Give yourself time. Don't judge. Practice patience, and most importantly, meditation. To assist you in that goal, here is a really positive exercise that can help refocus your inner dialogue:

1. **Pay attention to your limiting beliefs**. What are they? Write them down so that you can actually see them on paper.
2. **Start to dig deeper and investigate them**. Where is the repetition? What do they sound like?
3. **Think of how those beliefs are costing you.** As an example, let's say one of your limiting beliefs is that you're not fit enough to feel comfortable exercising in public at the gym. What's that (false) belief costing you? Your health, your well-being, your mood, years of life and possibly some health concerns that may not have manifested had you been exercising regularly. Pretty serious, huh! Limiting beliefs can be big or small, but all of them are affecting your life in some way.
4. **Now, come up with your *new* story.** Turn "I can't believe I'm divorced," to, "Now I'm free to begin a new life and open myself up to exciting new challenges and opportunities."
5. **Practice. Practice. Practice.** Change is a habit, not an event. And habits take practice. When limiting, negative or harmful self-talk rears its ugly head, stop what you're doing and focus on changing your internal story line. Do this as often as necessary.
6. **Practice some more!** Spend at least five minutes a day telling yourself your new story.

The Habitual Mindset and the Power of Transformation

Here's a short exercise to help curb your negative patterns of behavior and practice more mindful eating. This is more effective when I'm reading it to you in a video or recorded meditation instead of having you read it to yourself (with eyes open, of course), but we'll make the best of what we have right now! For those that want guided meditations to make the process a little easier, you can check out my MasterMind Meditations package at *LiveBlissNow.com*. For now, ideally you'd have someone read this to you as you try this short exercise. Then switch it up and read to the other person so that you can both practice. Ready?

> *Today our focus will be on your habitual patterns of behavior. Please sit comfortably and close your eyes. As we begin today, draw your attention to a pattern of behavior that we are changing. Our eating habits are undergoing a fundamental shift. Let's breathe for four complete breaths and recognize our courage for undertaking this fundamental change. Breathing in, we think courage; breathing out we think transformation. Again in, courage; and out, transformation. Again: courage, transformation. One last time: courage, transformation. Pause and slowly blink open your eyes once you're ready.*

We are all transforming every day. Our bodies are miraculous in that our cells are constantly renewing themselves. Our stomach lining actually transforms every 7 days. Think of yourself as a child; your body is not the same today as it was then. We are miraculous creatures, constantly changing, evolving and growing. As you recognize your body as it evolves, think about your patterns of thought. Are they the same? Do you notice that you get stuck in patterns that no longer serve you? As Lao Tzu says:

> *Watch your **thoughts**; they become **words**.*
> *Watch your **words**; they become **actions**.*
> *Watch your **actions**; they become **habits**.*
> *Watch your **habits**; they become **character**.*
> *Watch your **character**; it becomes your **destiny**.*

Today, think about yourself as you would like to be. Inhaling in, repeat your affirmation to yourself: "I am healthy," or however you would like to see yourself. Exhaling out, let go of the thoughts that no longer serve you. And let's take four complete rounds of breath together in silence. Go on, do it now!

Finally, realize that you may not be able to control what happens to you, but how you respond to what happens *is* within your control. We have the power to change our health. By treating our bodies with wisdom and compassion, we can change our lives.

Part 4

Your Environment

Oftentimes we think that our environment is merely the surroundings we live in: city or country, suburbia or downtown, coastal or landlocked. But increasingly, our environment plays a role—for better or worse—in how we live day-to-day.

Our environment consists of the air we breathe, the soil our food grows in, the water we drink and where our waste goes.

Beyond the physical stuff, the forests and the trees, the cities and the buildings, we live within our mental environment as well. That environment is created by the people we surround ourselves with, how they treat us, the messages they send us, as well as how we respond to their actions and behavior. Our mental and spiritual environment is also created by the social cues we pick up on from the general public, society as a whole and even the media.

All of our environments—physical, mental and spiritual—play a role in how we treat ourselves and our bodies. If you don't like where you are living physically, you may suppress your happiness with cupcakes and cookies. If you are cruel to yourself and your mental environment is a harsh one, you may turn to food as comfort, or you may use food to punish yourself. If your spiritual environment is empty, your soul may feel empty too. You might sulk on the couch feeling depressed for "no reason," shoveling in potato chips and chocolate bars. Our environments play a large role in how we feel about our lives and ourselves, which factors into how we treat our bodies.

When Visual Cues Aren't Enough

While we already know obesity is a huge problem in the US, other industrialized countries aren't in the same boat as us. France, for example, doesn't have an issue with obesity. Why? Author and award-winning researcher Brian Wansink, PhD, conducted an experiment to understand just that. He polled 282 people from Paris and Chicago and asked them when it was time to stop eating a meal.

The French reported that they stopped eating when "they no longer felt hungry." The Chicagoans stopped when "their plate was empty." Essentially the study revealed that the Chicagoans relied on external cues to tell them when to stop eating. Their external environment influenced how much they decided to eat, instead of listening to themselves.

Now consider how supersized our portions are here in the US. Visitors to our country marvel at how much food is included in an average "meal"—not just at home but in restaurants, too. Drinks, appetizers, bread, salad, main course, side dishes and dessert are standard for a big night out or a celebration meal—and for some, an average meal.

Once upon a time, the small hamburger that is now featured in the kids' meals at most fast food restaurants was the standard sandwich size for adults. Nowadays, burgers are doubled, even tripled, in size, and that's before the cheese, bacon, mayonnaise and ketchup are slathered on.

At home or out to dinner, we regularly load up our plates and then listen to our mother's voice in our head telling us to finish what's in front of us, regardless of how full we actually feel. What if we just used smaller plates and put less food on them to begin with?

What if we ate until we were full instead of until we were done licking the plate dry of every last morsel? For some, leaving food on the plate or in the bag or box can cause uncomfortable feelings of anxiety and lead us to think that we must compulsively eat until it's all gone. Next time, before shoveling all the remaining food into your mouth, stop. Recognize what's beginning to happen (anxiety), and realize that while uncomfortable at the moment, nothing bad will happen if you simply leave the food there and let the feeling pass.

Until we develop awareness of our body through our meditation practice, measuring out portions will be very important to curb overeating.

20 Minutes to Satiety

Our surroundings are also important when it comes to cues that we should stop eating. It takes about twenty minutes for our brains to register that our stomachs are full. The slower we eat, the easier it is for us not to overindulge.

In another experiment, Dr. Wansink created a section at Hardee's that was more relaxing than the rest of the fast food chain. He added jazz music, put down a white tablecloth and dimmed the lighting. Those in the atmospheric section ate an average of eleven minutes slower than those in the regular section, even though both were catering to the same lunchtime crowd.

So the next time you make yourself dinner, treat yourself right. Light some candles, set the table, put on your favorite relaxing music and take the time to really savor your food. You'll find that you slow down, chew more thoroughly, digest your food better and end up eating less—not to mention savor your food all the more. If you're simply on lunch break at work or having breakfast before leaving for the office, stop, slow down and make it enjoyable.

If the weather's nice, get outside and get some fresh air and sunshine while you eat. This lowers stress, in turn helping your body break down food more effectively so that you can actually make use of all the vital vitamins, minerals and nutrients.

You have the choice: to either make mealtime a fun, enjoyable time of day that you look forward to, or a stressful, hectic activity that leaves you with heartburn, indigestion or bloating. If you can't seem to stop and slow down for long enough to let your body do its job breaking down your food, then inevitably your digestion, and thus your health, will suffer. When you *enjoy* mealtime, you savor your food and eat simply for the nourishment that healthy food can provide, instead of using junky comfort foods to cheer you up or calm you down after a long day.

Un-Mindful Eating, or Eating While Unconscious

It's no secret that in these fast-paced fast food times, eating can often be an unconscious act. Have you ever eaten standing up or without awareness? Have you ever sat in front of the TV and devoured an entire meal or bowl of snacks without actually *tasting* a single ounce of it? What about eating while driving or at your desk? If you found yourself nodding in response to these questions, then you know the story all too well. The less time you take to pay attention to your food, to be conscious of actually eating it, the more junk you will likely eat and yet still be unsatisfied when you're done.

Practicing conscious eating is one way of practicing awareness, and it will help you cut back on overeating and bingeing, too. Other cultures practice conscious eating regularly. In Japan, there are tea ceremonies in which the ceremony or ritual is like a moving meditation. The whole process is not about drinking tea but about preparing a bowl of tea from one's heart and serving it from a generous spirit. The parts of the ceremony—the crisp linen, the bowls and mugs, the atmosphere of the room and the nodding and bowing—are as important, if not more so, than the contents of the tea pot itself. How do you think a cup of tea served from a traditional Japanese tea ceremony would taste compared to tea from a hot Styrofoam cup grabbed from the nearest convenient store? Not quite the same.

Eating With All Five Senses

Most cultures offer some form of thanks or appreciation before they eat. In the ancient Indian Ayurvedic tradition, practitioners are taught to eat with all five senses. Today, some 5,000 years later and with all the fast food restaurants in our culture, we can appreciate the value in this longstanding tradition more than ever. How to eat with all five senses? Here are a few ideas:

- **Eyes:** You may have heard the expression that we eat with our eyes, and as highly visual beings, this is very true. Food should not only look good but be prepared in a rainbow of colors, which makes it healthful as well as visually pleasing. The more colors in your food, the more nutrients are present, so think dark leafy greens, red cherries, purple berries, green, orange and yellow peppers and the like. Different pigments of color each indicate the presence of certain antioxidants and phytochemicals, so whenever you see (naturally) colorful food, dig in! Also helpful to the eye is putting your food on a smaller plate so that you don't feel the need to fill up a larger plate with lots of food that you're not even hungry for.
- **Ears:** Play your favorite soothing music in the background while you eat. Studies have shown that the faster the tempo, the more we eat. Relaxing music actually helps us relax and properly digest our food.
- **Nose:** Our body starts to prepare for digestion based on the foods we smell. Our sense of smell is also largely associated with how food tastes. Let yourself take in the aroma of food cooking so that your body can better prepare for digestion.
- **Taste:** Ayurvedic tradition suggests that we eat foods that are a combination of sweet, sour, salty, bitter, pungent and astringent. All of these tastes not only prevent food cravings

by giving us all the tastes that the body craves, but they also help us get in touch with our body's innate wisdom as it tells us which nutrients we are lacking.

- **Touch:** Get re-acquainted with your food. Instead of picking up a slice of pizza and shoving it down your throat without a second thought, try slowing down and using a knife and fork to cut it up into smaller, more manageable portions that take longer to eat. Or, try finger foods so that you can actually touch the food that's about to become a part of your body. If it sounds pretty intimate, that's because it is—you are what you eat! Sometimes we become so distant from what we're eating that we become disconnected, and thus apathetic, towards it. Try getting acquainted with your food again, and you may find that you start caring a bit more about what you put into your mouth.
- **Putting it all together:** Next time you pick up a peach, don't just bite right into it without taking a second glance or giving it a second thought. Feel the fuzzy skin, notice the texture, the wonderful sweet aroma as you bring the peach to your nose. As you bite into it, how does it taste? Linger over the sensory experience—the touch and feel of the peach's skin and flesh, the sweet smell, the juicy sound as you bite into it. Cover all the senses—sight, sound, smell, taste and touch—if you can. When you become fully present and aware while eating, you'll find that you slow down, relax, appreciate and enjoy your food that much more. After all, isn't that what it's all about?

Our Planet is Just an Extension of Our Bodies

It can be so easy to eat without giving much thought as to what exactly we're eating. Let's face it: many of us are guilty of shoveling food into our mouths without any clue as to where it came from or how it got to our refrigerator. This disconnection from our food and the mindless, unconscious eating that results has a lot to do with why so many of us are overweight and unhealthy.

We know that on a physical level, we are completely connected to our environment, because the air we breathe and the food that nourishes us gives us the vitality we need to live healthy and happy lives.

We must eat, breathe, drink and move around in our surroundings merely to survive, so to think that we can separate or distance ourselves from it is crazy. Our bodies are an extension of our environment. So if you think of it that way, where do you think all those chemicals, pesticides and toxins we pollute the earth with are bound to end up?

Dirt: *More than Meets the Eye*

Even beyond the issue of dangerous toxins and chemicals building up all around us, we have another problem on our hands: the slow but steady depletion of our soil's essential minerals—the ones we need to be strong and healthy.

Many trace minerals that are absolutely vital to our health are found in soil, which then make their way into our plant foods and then our bodies, in the form of lettuce in our salads, tomatoes on our burgers and onions in our frittatas.

These essential minerals are the fuel our bodies need to grow, to fight off disease, to live and breathe, to run and jump, to work and to play. The term "essential" means that we cannot produce these on our own, so we must get them from our food. And when you consider that our main source of minerals (soil) is being depleted of the very thing we need, that is cause for concern!

Just in case the term 'mineral' is a little foggy, just a few of the key minerals include calcium, magnesium, sodium, potassium, selenium and zinc. Although these are just a handful of the many minerals we need, these all serve such a crucial role in our bodies and our health. Calcium, as you know, is important for bone health, but it also reduces cramps, helps with sleep and protects against colon cancer. But too much is not a good thing, which is why we need calcium's inseparable partner, magnesium.

Magnesium is crucial for balancing the calcium in our bodies, helping us to better utilize what we need and get rid of the excess—which can damage our precious arteries and give us high blood pressure. So many of us are deficient in magnesium, especially in these high-stress times, as stress depletes our magnesium levels at an even higher rate. This essential mineral is so important for relaxation—for our bodies, blood vessels and muscles. It inevitably helps with sleep, too, and can help lower high blood pressure caused by high calcium levels.

Potassium is essential for heart regularity and for improving cell and nerve conduction, while selenium is a powerful antioxidant that helps prevent cancer and is vital for thyroid and sex hormone production.

Zinc's importance can't be overstated, either. It's crucial for our immune strength, mental clarity, a healthy appetite, reproductive development, prostate health and many enzyme systems. These are only a few of the key minerals we need, but I'm sure you're beginning to see the bigger picture of why they are so darn important.

Without healthy mineral-rich soils that are free of pesticides, herbicides and chemicals, our bodies would have a much harder time getting all the nutrients we need. Problem is, our soils have *already* lost so many of the minerals we need, so it requires us to supplement our diet—however healthy—with a multi-vitamin and multi-mineral supplement.

Decades ago, humans could get all the nutrients they needed simply from eating foods grown from the mineral-rich earth. That's not the case these days, and the situation is only bound to get worse—unless we put our foot down.

The Problems with Mass Production

Before we had factory farms that were specifically designed for mass production, farmers planted crops that were fertilized by cow manure from the cows that grazed on the land. Today, that image exists mostly just in marketing materials—rarely on farms, as we'd like to think. The idealized picture of this pure, organic process is not at all the reality that exists in the mass production of our food-like products today.

A good example of this reality can be found in Michael Pollan's book, *The Omnivore's Dilemma*. The book follows a cow from the farm lot where it's raised, to the slaughterhouse where it's killed for consumption. What readers come to understand throughout the book is that the mass production of beef, poultry and pork, while a very profitable system of raising animals for food, is unfortunately chock-full of problems that can't be ignored. Raising just *one cow* produces more methane—which is 23 times more potent than carbon dioxide as a contributor to global warming—than is even produced by a car in a day! And it's only predicted to get worse. The FDA predicts a 60 percent increase in methane produced from agriculture by 2030.

The problems extend beyond the mass production of meat alone. The attempt to make every food production system as efficient as it can be, at the cost of our health, results in other atrocities. The more and more fertilizer, pesticides and herbicides that we use on grass for grazing animals and for the produce you and I eat, the more we deplete the all-important nutrients in our soil—the nutrients, as we mentioned, that are absolutely vital to our health and well-being.

Pesticides are used to kill the "bugs" that eat our plants, yet we are expected to eat the plants along with the bug-killing chemicals. If it destroys any insect that crosses its path, how safe can these chemicals be for us to consume on a daily basis? Not to mention, pesticides threaten the nutritional values of the very plants they were created to "protect."

Chemical fertilizers are made from non-renewable resources such as natural gas and coal, which unfortunately feed the plant but starve the soil. With continued use, the soil's structure breaks down by the depletion of worms and microorganisms. Not good, right? And we're just not just sprinkling this stuff around cautiously. No, we're being more than generous with it—more than *100 million tons* generous. According to the Food and Agriculture Organization of the United Nations, the world's nitrogen fertilizer demand is expected to increase from 105 million tons to almost 113 million tons in 2015. That's an annual growth rate of 1.7 percent.

Not only is it affecting our soils, but that nitrogen also makes its way into our streams, rivers and oceans, where it starts to wreak major havoc, creating uninhabitable areas known as dead zones. These areas have zero or close to zero oxygen, killing all the fish and other oxygen-dependent organisms that once lived in it.

To better understand the severity of the situation, the United Nations Environment Programme reported that to date, there are 150 such zones in the world. They are primarily off the east coast of the US, as well as in Europe, and range in length from 1 to 46,000 miles. Yikes!

Mercury: *It's Not Just a Planet Anymore*

Now let's talk about mercury poisoning. This is something that most of us have heard a lot about in recent years, mostly in reports warning us to cut back our consumption of tuna and some other fish because of their high mercury levels.

The explanation that seems to best show us how tuna and certain other fish have become a health risk is a quote from a December 2011 article from the *Scientific American*: "Human industrial activity (such as coal-fired electricity generation, smelting and the incineration of waste) ratchets up the amount of airborne mercury, which eventually finds its way into lakes, rivers and the ocean, where it is gobbled up by unsuspecting fish and other marine life."

As I stated earlier, we are all connected to the environment. Like a ripple effect, everything we do affects something or someone. Likewise, everything that's done to the environment affects us as well.

It works like this: small fish are eaten by bigger fish, and the bigger fish are eaten by even bigger fish. Mercury accumulates throughout this entire life cycle. By the time you get to the bigger fish—tuna, swordfish, shark and the like—the mercury levels have become quite high. So when we eat the tuna, we are eating all the accumulated mercury along with it.

Even worse is when you consider that mercury is the second most toxic substance in the world, right next to plutonium. This is what we are ingesting and feeding our children when we eat canned tuna and other high-mercury fish!

When mercury gets into our bodies, it's not a pretty picture. Dr. Oz sums it up best on his website: "When mercury gets into our bloodstream, it goes right to our brain and attacks our nervous system. Left untreated, it can cause permanent neuropsychiatric brain damage, learning disorders in children, autoimmune disease, and even heart problems." Not good!

Mercury: *My Family's Journey*

My oldest son, my pride and joy, gave my life magic. When he smiled, he was pure goodness. His trusting nature, beautiful smile and outgoing personality touched anyone he came in contact with.

But as I picked up the phone that day, I felt a sinking sensation. I had been out of town for 10 days. I was jet-lagged and looking forward to having dinner with my kids. As I saw the school number in the caller ID window, I answered with fear.

"Mrs. Goldberg?" said the woman on the other end of the line. "Are you available for an afternoon meeting?"

"Of course," I replied, scheduling a half-hour block for later that day. As I got to school an hour before the kids got out for the afternoon, I felt like I was the one being called to the principal's office.

As the principal began to explain my son's behavior, I wasn't surprised. In a sense I felt relieved to have someone who was an expert explain. He had ADHD. That was the staff consensus. His constant fidgeting, his inability to sit still and impulsiveness was getting him into trouble at school.

Four and a half million children have ADHD in the US. Two and a half million are on medication. These drugs are amphetamines. They are appetite suppressants. They can cause depression, insomnia, motor disorders. The cherry on top of all that: my son *hated* how the drugs made him feel.

Still, the diagnosis wasn't exactly the solution the principal seemed to think it was. *Don't you know what he's been through?* I wanted to yell at her. *Can't you see that his parents just got divorced?*

Above all, I wanted to protect my son from her cold, almost clinical assessment. I understood him best. My heart broke for him, and yet I felt powerless to protect him. My high-energy little boy, with his desire to please everyone, was being crushed every time he ran into rules that he seemed destined to break. He didn't act deliberately; he would just act impulsively and then get into trouble.

It is really stressful for kids who have to control their behavior. They know that they are not meeting the expectations of their parents or their teachers. They want to please us but sometimes they just can't help themselves.

Each reprimand was one more insult, one more sling and arrow lodged against his already shaky and quite vulnerable self-esteem. Each time he was told he was a "trouble maker," that was just one more label that he seemed destined to live up to. After awhile, it was all he had to hold onto.

My shoulders sagged from the responsibility. I felt overwhelmed for him and for myself. He needed extra help, that much was clear.

Extra tutoring, medication, a psychologist. He had grown 12 inches in the last year alone. Suddenly, my "little" six-year-old boy looked ten. People saw this tall beautiful boy and assumed he was older. The same behavior that is okay for a six-year-old wasn't acceptable for a ten-year-old, even if he only "looked" ten.

At school, the other kids were afraid of him. He looked different. He didn't understand his own strength. One time, he broke a little girl's arm from playing a little too roughly. When the school called to tell me, I worried for the little girl, but mostly I worried for my little boy. He didn't get it. He just felt people's anger directed at him, which made him feel clumsy, bad and stupid.

So that was that. It had been decreed by the school principal and the staff, so ADHD it was. My baby started medication. Ritalin. It didn't work. He lost his appetite. He couldn't sleep. School was still challenging, but now his beautiful unrestrained personality was dampened. He was sullen, morose. Though, I imagine, his teachers were happier because now he was easier to manage. I imagine it was like teaching a zombie.

I asked the doctor if this was normal. I was told that it was and that I should keep him on the medication. So I trusted the doctors. And the school. These were professionals who knew more than me, right? They were experts. They must know best. Once again, I relinquished my power. As doubt gnawed at me, I made myself ignore it and turned my cheek the other way.

So what role does mercury play in all this? Well, consider this: in America, one in six children has been exposed to mercury levels so high that they are potentially at risk for developing learning disabilities, motor skill impairment, short-term memory loss and other neurological issues—like ADHD.

According to a 2005 article from the Public Broadcasting Service, "One government analysis shows that 630,000 children each year are exposed to potentially unsafe mercury levels in the womb." And in a 2012 study that looked at data from roughly 600 mothers and their children, researchers reported that the kids exposed to higher mercury levels in the womb were more likely to have attention problems, hyperactivity and other ADHD symptoms at age 8.

Was I just another statistic? Was my son? Was our lifestyle, our environment, to blame for his ADHD? Would he be forever tainted, doomed to a life of medication, because I tried to make sure he had enough fish in his diet growing up?

While I eventually learned that there was no point in engaging in the "what if's" and "why me's," I did learn how my son and I could better manage his ADHD: meditation. The wonderful cure-all!

In a landmark study conducted by Dr. Sarina Grosswald, EdD, she reported that having students meditate for just 10 minutes twice a day reduced their stress by 50 to 53 percent. There was an overall improvement in attention by 19 percent, and a 13 percent improvement in executive functioning. The students became more open and responsive to learning, and were better able to self-monitor.

How is meditation so effective? By helping with:

1. **Physical symptoms like stress**
2. **Emotional well-being**
3. **Spiritual well-being**

Meditation can also help parents not be so reactive. It is stressful to have a child who is constantly getting into trouble, forgetting deadlines, losing their belongings and acting impulsively. Frustration or anger just makes their already fragile self-esteem worse. It's much better to accept who they are and try to facilitate. Meditation is the inner reserve that makes that possible.

Parents who have kids with ADHD often feel frustrated and at the end of their rope. And then they feel guilty for having those feelings. In addition to having to educate a sometimes defiant or difficult child, parents often end up having to advocate for their child at school so that he or she receives the compassion and extra help they require. This can be very difficult emotionally at times. But thankfully we have meditation. It helps us to release painful emotions and recharge from a stressful day. Next time you feel at the end of your rope, sit down and do a 10-minute meditation—or more, if you're feeling up to it! If you're not sure where to start and would like some extra guidance, I created a guided meditation package called MasterMind Meditations, which you can check out at *LiveBlissNow.com*.

Courage in the Face of Fear

"Courage is being scared to death and doing the right thing anyway."
~ Chae Richardson

Our single most important job as parents is to raise happy, independent, resilient kids who feel like they can accomplish anything. Although fitting in at school is important, more important is to send the message that "*You are okay no matter what. Who you are, what you think and how you act is all good with me.*"

Accepting that your child's way may be different than yours but no less important or valid is the definition of true, unconditional love. In my desire to sync my son's world with the school system, I lost sight of the environment we were creating for him.

Toxicity comes not only from our exterior environment (the physical world we live in), but also from the messages that we receive along the way. Crushing our spirit is far more dangerous to our development than missing a homework deadline or showing up late. Each time we give our children the opportunity to excel, we empower them. As I learned to shift my focus onto the areas that my son *could* excel, he began to feel empowered. Learning that he could control some elements of his environment, he began to shine.

After breaking that girl's arm by accident, my son felt clumsy and untrustworthy. We knew he was still inherently gentle and kind, but other kids became fearful. To demonstrate to him how much we trusted him with others, we got him a puppy. He was so loving with the puppy and so gentle that the stigma of having hurt someone quickly lost its sting. He realized that accidents happen, but that his didn't have to define him.

His curiosity and sense of adventure often got him into trouble. We channeled that curiosity by sending him to Ecuador to build schools and teach children how to speak English. Each time he helped another human being learn and grow, his own self-esteem grew as well.

He often forgets things and can be disorganized. We use examples of great business leaders who knew their strengths and focused on them instead of their weakness. Sir Richard Branson is a great example of someone who had ADHD and managed to turn his liability into an asset. His constant lack of attention and need for stimulation led to his incredible creativity and countless endeavors.

My son has been one of my greatest teachers. He has taught me to let go of my own ego and my need for him to do things "my way." As he has struggled with adversity, he has shown wisdom far beyond his years. Although school is still challenging for him, his intelligence and creativity help him to find solutions. He has the courage and determination that often come from learning early on that life will be tough sometimes, but if you hang in there, everything will be fine.

The Butterfly Effect: *The Environment Connection*

As you can see, we are inescapably connected to the environment in which we live, and unfortunately, we cannot be truly healthy on a sick planet. Every single change in our environment, big or small, affects us in ways we cannot even imagine. The more you understand this, the easier it will be to tackle this challenge and change your life.

Some of the things you have read in this book may upset you the way they did for me when I first learned about how our world seems to be falling apart all around us. It can be daunting to say the least, and may even make you question what difference you can possibly make by changing to a plant-based diet.

David Pimentel, a professor of ecology and agriculture at Cornell University, suggests that if people became vegetarians, it would reduce the total energy inputs in our food system by about a third. For vegans, who don't eat dairy or eggs in addition to no meat or fish, the energy consumption would be reduced by about 50 percent compared to conventional consumption.

If you want to know for certain that the changes to your diet will not only impact your health but also that of our planet, consider the butterfly effect. No, I'm not talking about that movie with Ashton Kutcher, but rather the findings of a study by Edward Lorenz, a mathematician and meteorologist at MIT.

Lorenz found that a butterfly flapping its wings in South America could affect the weather in New York's Central Park. This was coined "the butterfly effect," and it showed that small changes in one place could lead to larger changes somewhere else.

While this has huge implications for our environment as a whole, it can also be incredibly empowering on a smaller, more personal scale. If a tiny butterfly can affect change in the world, just imagine what you can do! Making the decision to adopt a whole foods plant-based diet has more far-reaching effects than you may even be able to imagine, but you can be sure that the impact will be felt not only by you, but also by your family, your loved ones and ultimately, the planet.

Part 5

Your Relationships

Relationships matter. Agreed? Ok this chapter is over. Just kidding. Many people say that they believe relationships are important, but their actions say otherwise. That's precisely the problem.

The collective bond between two or more people has a real, significant and beneficial impact on everyone involved. And the stronger the relationship, the more beneficial the impact.

Think of your strongest relationships: the laughter you've shared, the shoulders you've cried on, the gifts you've given and received, the quiet moments, the loud and boisterous ones. Now picture your life without those people, those friends and family, coworkers and colleagues, neighbors and roommates.

Imagine a world where you lived a solitary existence, with yourself as your only company. No shoulder to cry on, no one to make you laugh or think about things a different way, no one to wrap birthday presents for or open them from, no one to celebrate holidays with or share a quiet meal or fun cocktail party with. No one to check up on your progress, congratulate your successes, console your failures or applaud your advances. Every pound you lost, every meal you cooked, every workout you completed, it would just be you, and only you, to witness your triumph or defeat.

Chances are you're depressed just thinking about it! And there's your evidence: the mere thought of your strongest relationships improves your life, while just thinking about losing those relationships is enough to get you down.

My Strongest Relationships, My Greatest Teachers

My own relationships have been both a source of tremendous comfort and joy, as well incredible pain. As much as I love the happy times, the painful ones helped me grow the most.

Relationships give us feedback. In our own vacuum, we tell ourselves all kinds of stories about ourselves, and of course we believe them because who is there to second-guess us? But interpersonal relationships give us the opportunity to practice our skills and see if we are on track.

At my mother's shiva (the Jewish ritual for mourning), all of her friends were there to support us. They brought us food so that we wouldn't have to think about cooking, they told wonderful stories so that we could remember her, and best of all, they gave us the ability to get outside ourselves during those painful moments of grief. After all, if you have no choice but to get up, get dressed, interact with others and function with humanity, then you *have* to keep going. Being surrounded by loved ones helped me heal.

Each time my family and I heard a story about our mother, it broadened our perspective of her life. We saw how many people she touched and realized just how special she was. We also got the feeling that she was still alive. After all, her memories, her values and her humor were now internalized in others, so her spirit was still around us. As we further incorporated her values into our own inner dialogues, we added another dimension to ourselves. As a result, we became that much more whole, and that much better for having known her.

At first I was angry that someone only fifty-four-years-old had to die. It seemed so unfair. I knew so many unhappy people who would almost rather be dead, so many seventy-five-year-olds who hated their life. My mother had wanted to live so badly. She appreciated every day, and lived with so much zest and energy. Then I realized that her gift to me had been showing me how to do just that—how to *really* live.

Rather than focus on the fact that I couldn't share life with her physically, I began to practice sharing it with her spiritually. I saw that the true way to honor her life, her wisdom and her values was to try to incorporate those meaningful aspects into my own life.

It didn't happen overnight. At first, everything that my mother stood for gave me too much pain to deal with. She was the matriarch and had valued family, and yet I was too angry at my brothers and father to have them as a part of my life at the time. But then I remembered how well she had forgiven my father, and so I vowed to practice. Eventually, I saw how forgiveness toward others ended up helping me.

There is a great Buddhist expression that says, "Holding on to anger is like grasping a hot coal with the intent of throwing it at someone else; you are the one who gets burned."

I missed the connection to my mother, and angry or not, having my family around kept a part of her alive. Forgiving them became a gift to myself; I could finally drop those hot coals of anger and let my hands, and my heart, heal.

My mother loved helping others. She had spent a lifetime doing just that. In retrospect, I had spent a lifetime helping myself. I only had this realization while at my first yoga retreat. Our retreat leaders had us introduce ourselves by answering the question, "Please tell us the last time you did something for someone else." I was mortified. As we went around the circle, everyone else, it seemed, had in some way been actively contributing.

I had always been raised to be charitable, and I could have easily described lots of contribution checks I had written, but had I actually made helping others a part of my daily life? Obviously, not so much. I had the mistaken belief that there was a finite amount of love, money and success to go around, and that by competing with others,

I would ensure that I would be successful and happy. It turns out I had it all wrong.

According to research done by Harvard University Associate Professor of Business Administration Michael Norton, spending money on others actually makes you happier than spending money on yourself. Norton points to research that supports the theory that money spent on ourselves can often leave us feeling empty and remorseful, but the opposite is true when we spend on others—be it our family, friends or charity.

What I didn't understand is how connected we all are. Adi Shankara, an 8th-century yogi, described our separate-ness as an illusion. To demonstrate his point, let's look at an example. Let's say you eat an apple. You may think it's just you and the apple. But in reality, it's you *plus* the farmer that grew the apple, the person that harvested it, the driver that took it from the orchard to the market and the guy that sold it to me. All of these people are mutually connected to that one piece of fruit.

The illusion that we are alone and operate in a vacuum is just that—an illusion. The next time you feel distant or alone, remember the many layers of connection you actually have.

Turning Around the Negative

My mother valued marriage. She probably would have been appalled to see me in the throes of a divorce. As my life was dismantled, not only did I lose a life partner, but the world as I knew it shattered. Our community of couples no longer made sense for me as a newly single person, and I felt like an outsider at all the favorite places we used to go. The social upheaval was almost worse than the divorce itself.

But instead of focusing on everything I hated about the situation, I started to look at the lessons I could get from the pain. As my identity as a "good daughter" and a "good wife" disintegrated, I learned to relax and accept that my sense of self as a stagnant entity was also just an illusion, one that was also constantly changing, evolving and growing over time. Who I was now was not the end of the line, just as who I was then did not define who I was now. Who could tell what the future held?

This much I did know: the old me was allowing a new me to unfold. I had been creating needless suffering over things I couldn't control, and by holding on too tightly to old habits and relationships, I wouldn't be able to allow new ones into my life. But that was all changing now.

Conscious Communication

Once I had a shift in perspective, I had to relearn how to communicate what I wanted from my father—instead of expecting him to intuitively know (he's not a mind-reader, who knew?!). Rather than reacting to him with anger and resentment, I learned how to communicate consciously and with awareness.

Marshall Rosenberg, the psychologist who developed Nonviolent Communication, explains a few ways that we can reframe and change our perspective to prevent anger and resentment in communication:

1. **Avoid words that reinforce a sense of victimization**. "I am abandoned, rejected, unloved. My father deserted our family for someone new."
2. **Outline the facts as if you were an outside observer without any bias.** "My father is in a new relationship."
3. **Identify the feeling.** "I feel afraid of being left out."
4. **Identify the need.** "I need to feel connection and love."
5. **Ask for what you want.** "I would like to have dinner this week with the whole family." Make sure that this is framed as a request, not a demand.

Today, my father is a vital, loving part of my life. He is present and participates in my children's upbringing. I know that he cares and loves me, and I respect his new relationship and am truly grateful that he is cared for and happy.

Now I am simply grateful for the wonderful people in my life. Each person has touched me in different and unique ways—teaching me, supporting me and changing me. In turn, I have been able to do the same for them. As Rumi said, "No mirror ever became iron again; No bread ever became wheat; No ripened grape ever became sour fruit. Mature yourself and be secure from a change for the worse. Become the light."

I see now how my mother was able to have so many diverse people in her life: she never judged anybody. She accepted people unconditionally and felt blessed to contribute to them in any way she could. As a result, her life was rich with love, friendships and connections. When romantic love failed her, she found other ways to experience love and connection.

The Gallup organization's director Tom Rath believes that we are all aware of the value of friendship, especially during difficult times. In his book, *Vital Friends: The People You Can't Afford To Live Without*, Rath makes the point that if you ask people why they became homeless, why their marriage failed or why they continue to overeat time and time again, they often say it is because of the poor quality or nonexistence of friendships. They feel outcast and unloved.

Rath undertook a massive study of friendship alongside several leading researchers. Their work resulted in some surprising statistics: if your best friend eats healthfully, you are five times more likely to have a healthy diet yourself.

Married people say that friendship is more than five times as important as physical intimacy within marriage. Those who say they have no real friends at work have only a one in twelve chance of feeling engaged at their job. Conversely, if you have a best friend at work, you are seven times more likely to feel engaged.

Clearly, be it personally or professionally, physically or spiritually, relationships really matter.

It Takes a Village: *Hardwick, Vermont, and the Collective Conscience*

Relationships matter across a variety of spectrums. They can have commercial, economic and even professional impacts. Case in point: Hardwick, Vermont.

Like many small American towns in recent years, Hardwick has seen jobs leaving, stores closing and businesses folding. But a small collective of farmers, entrepreneurs, businesspeople and forward thinkers are banding together to not only enjoy individual success, but collective progress as well.

In a 2008 article for the *New York Times*, reporter Marian Burros noted that, "Cooperation takes many forms. Vermont Soy stores and cleans its beans at High Mowing, which also lends tractors to High Fields, a local compositing company. Byproducts of High Mowing's operation—pumpkins and squash that have been smashed to extract seeds—are now being purchased by Pete's Greens and turned into soup. Along with 40,000 pounds of squash and pumpkin, Pete's bought 2,000 pounds of High Mowing's cucumbers this year and turned them into pickles."

One is the Loneliest Number

You can't (nor should you) do it alone. It's important to have self-awareness, to be independent and able to stand on your own two feet, but the simple truth is that life is meant to be shared.

From the beginning of time, humans, even animals, have existed in packs, groups, families and shared collectives. During our hunting and gathering days, being part of a group meant safety in numbers. And more hunters meant more food, providing not only for themselves but also for those who weren't able to hunt. The hunters delivered the food to those who could prepare it, using tools that were crafted by others in the group. Each person did his or her part, and the group's survival depended on their collective strength.

Later on, as humans evolved, we did so together, roaming like nomads across the early continents or behind stone walls of the planet's earliest cities. Since then, our intense desire to form groups has evolved along with the rest of civilization. What are Facebook and Twitter but evidence of our continuing evolution to seek out like-minded people to relate to and engage with? To connect with friends and family even if we can't be with them in person?

The fact is, strong, rooted relationships aren't just a luxury but one of life's necessities. Did you know, for instance, that having strong relationships affects your risk of mortality as much as smoking and drinking do, and even *more* than obesity?

In a study on social relationships and mortality risk done for the Department of Psychology at Brigham Young University, researchers Julianne Holt-Lunstad, Timothy B. Smith and Bradley Layton took the results of 148 studies on social relationships and found that the people with strong social relationships were 50 percent more likely to live longer than their socially reclusive counterparts.

According to the study, a lack of friends is as damaging as smoking 15 cigarettes a day or being an alcoholic, and it's twice as damaging as obesity and more harmful than not exercising. Study author Holt-Lunstad said, "We need to start taking our social relationships just as seriously we take these other factors."

Finding Strength in Support Groups

Relationships and support are particularly important when you are starting something new. Change is rarely easy, so anything we can do to help strengthen our resolve or stay the course is usually welcome when the opportunity for change presents itself.

While the determination, perseverance and results will be up to you, it doesn't hurt to get a little help from your friends along the way. Did you know that people do better—be it with overcoming addiction, getting healthy, sticking to an exercise plan or simply trying to be a better person—when they have a partner or a group that they can share their challenges with?

According to the American Psychological Association article "Teaming Up to Drop Pounds" by Charlotte Huff, "Studies have demonstrated that a variety of group treatment settings—from intensive closed groups in a university clinic to more commercial-style programs like Weight Watchers—can help people achieve at least some weight loss and can prove more effective than dieting alone."

The results of a study by the Agricultural Research Service discovered that dieters who "...have the help of a support group may experience less stress and less of a brainpower drain than those who go it alone."

The Top 10 Benefits of Relationships

Let's dig deeper into why strong personal bonds matter so much by exploring these top ten benefits of relationships:

1. **A friend in need**. Friends come in all shapes and sizes, but the best quality of a friend is that they know when you need them. It's often our default setting to put on a brave face and greet the world with a smile, even when our world is crumbling around us. But friends care and know us well enough to look beyond the façade and reach out when we need a helping hand. Friends can be the difference between succeeding at a new venture and failing miserably.
2. **Care and convenience**. Like a convenience store, our best relationships are open twenty-four hours a day, seven days a week, 365 days a year. And they are often as close as a phone call, tweet or text away!
3. **In times of doubt**. Doubt is a progress killer. Doubt can make us lose our way, question ourselves and derail even our

best plans. When in doubt, strong relationships can make us stronger. Think of how often a good friend, family member or colleague has talked you out of a bad decision by reminding you how strong you really are.

4. **Giving is receiving**. We are in a dynamic exchange with the universe. When we give love and affection, it comes right back to us. When we are generous with our heart and even our finances, a sense of abundance is created, which tends to find its way back into our lives. Unlike a zero sum game, where looking out for #1 is the objective, this works like an upward spiral with no limits. A simple act of kindness to another will tend to result in further acts of kindness by them to others, and so on. For example, have you ever noticed that, when driving, if someone slows down to let you merge ahead of them, you will be more likely to allow someone to merge in front of you? Conversely, if people keep speeding up to prevent you from merging in, it creates a sense of "survival of the fittest," and you will probably react accordingly.
5. **Laughter is the best medicine**. Who can make us laugh like our close and trusted circle of friends? And when you consider how healthy laughter is in boosting our mood (and physical health), this is one benefit that should be hard to forget.
6. **Strength in numbers**. Going at it alone can make us weak. The constant pressure of change and the insecurity and doubt of trying something new can wear us down if we're not careful. Picking up the phone and talking to a friend, texting a buddy or simply chatting with a friend or neighbor can instantly provide us with strength that we may not be able to summon on our own.
7. **Support makes us strong**. It would be nice if life were full of straight roads and no detours, but we all know that will never be the case. Human nature is such that we have highs and lows, peaks and valleys, ups and downs. When we get

weak, which is a frequent side effect of trying new things and forging new paths, having a strong support system can make us strong again or simply give us the boost in mood we need to make it through.

8. **Perspective is power**. One of the side effects of trying to do everything alone is that in isolation, perspective can be hard to come by. Our mind, often full of the cruel words and labels from our childhood insecurities, can become sidetracked when left to its own devices. We can build ourselves up or down, talk ourselves into or out of projects and decisions; but the simple objectivity of a fresh pair of eyes, provided by a trusted friend, colleague or family member, can often provide the right amount of perspective to make the right decisions.
9. **Deadlines and due dates**. Starting a project is relatively simple, but sticking with it through the end can be difficult—and for some of us, an insurmountable challenge—if we try to do it alone. Having friends to keep us on top of due dates and deadlines, to chart our progress or remind us of how far we have to go, can prove to be the support we need to reach our goals when we might have given up otherwise.
10. **Together is better**. Facing tough times, challenges or obstacles together simply feels better. Even the good stuff feels that much better when you have someone to share it with! Next time you have a challenge coming up—be it a change in diet or exercise routine, a 5K race, the Get Blissed 21-Day Challenge or anything in between—see if you can enlist a friend or family member to support you along the way. Better yet, see if they'll do it with you! The already enriching experience will be doubly so with others involved.

So now that we realize how important it is to have people you can count on, let's learn some techniques to help us keep those relationships healthy.

I'm sure you're probably already familiar with the story of *The Wizard of Oz*, but just to be sure, here is a brief synopsis. Dorothy is from Kansas. One day, she is swept away in a tornado and transported to the land of Oz. Upon her arrival, her house lands on the Wicked Witch of the East, instantly killing her. The people of the land are all very happy about this, as the witch had terrorized them for years.

The ruler of the land, Glinda, takes the magical ruby slippers off the evil witch and gives them to Dorothy. Then the witches' other sister, the Wicked Witch of the West, shows up and demands the slippers. Upon finding out they'd been given to Dorothy, the witch threatens her.

Dorothy asks how she can get home and is told to find the Wizard of Oz in Emerald City. Along the way to find him, the Wicked Witch of the West and Dorothy have many conflicts, as the witch tries to get the shoes. The wizard tells Dorothy that he will only help her get home if she kills the Wicked Witch of the West and brings him her broom. So that's what Dorothy does, and she is finally able to return home.

This story was one of my favorites growing up. I would watch it year after year, cheering for Dorothy and being terrified of the Wicked Witch. A couple of years ago, I saw the play *Wicked,* and it changed my appreciation for the film.

In *Wicked*, we meet Elphaba, the Wicked Witch of the West. She is green, and we learn how difficult it was for her growing up and being so different from everyone else. We also meet Glinda, a beautiful, popular blonde who terrorizes her. We see Elphaba, a social outcast competing for social status, and recognize how difficult it is to be Elphaba. And we begin to understand the fierce rivalry between the two. We see Elphaba struggle with her looks, her career and her relationships, and we begin to develop empathy for her instead of a simplistic good versus evil. As we view her life with a broader perspective, we are able to become more tolerant and develop more understanding of who she is and why she does the things she does.

This process of taking a step back and looking at things in a completely new way is similar to what you will hopefully experience as you begin to meditate. During meditation, we develop the role of the witnessing observer, where we can distance ourselves from our thoughts and feelings and better observe our behavior without the bias. As we learn to take ourselves out of the day-to-day drama, we are able to stop taking things so personally.

Taking Steps Forward

As you can probably tell by now, the strength of your relationships is absolutely vital for a healthy, blissful life—so much so that I've built this facet into the Get Blissed 21-Day Challenge, for those that are moving forward with the challenge following this book. Here are some simple things you can do to enlist your strongest friends, coworkers, neighbors, roommates or family members to help you with as you begin the challenge:

- **Email five friends or coworkers about your decision to start the Get Blissed 21-Day Challenge.** Feel free to use our "Letter to Friends," which is available for download at *LiveBlissNow.com*. It's printed at the end of this section as well.
- **Research has shown that just making a public declaration of your intention—whatever it may be—will make you more likely to stick to the program.**
- **Ask if anyone would like to join you in your challenge.**
- **Arrange to split up some meals with your friends.**
- **Decide who will make which meals, and then share the cooking as well as the finished meal.** If you are doing this with co-workers, brown bag lunches can be an easy way to share the responsibility.
- **Choose one night during the week that you can get together and have a cooking party.** My friends and I like

to call it our "Gourmet Club!" Bring re-sealable containers and have everyone exchange meals.

- **Put on some great music, laugh, dance and let loose!**
- **Join our online community to share your struggles, questions, success stories and everything in between.** The places to connect with us online are on our Facebook page, at Facebook.com/LiveBlissNow; on the Live Bliss Now website, at *LiveBlissNow.com*; or on Twitter, at @LiveBlissNow. We'd love to hear from you!

Letter to Friends:

Feel free to change the wording as you please!

Dear ________,

I am taking back my health. I will be doing the *Get Blissed Challenge* for 21 days to do just that. During these 21 days, I pledge to eat whole plant-based foods to nourish my body and mind. I will be emphasizing natural foods that come from the earth, not a laboratory (packaged foods with a "natural" label don't count!).

I would appreciate your support during this time. If you care to join me in this challenge and enjoy some delicious food together, I will be hosting a cooking party on ________. Bring re-sealable containers so we can all take home meals!

I would love to share this journey with you, cook together and support each other, but if you're not up to it, I would love your support either way during these 21 days. Thanks for hearing me out!

Sincerely,
(Your name)

Part 6

Your Spirit

We are each born into this world with a unique spiritual nature. Our soul is truly like a fingerprint, full of twists and turns, lefts and rights and whirls and patterns that no other human on this planet can duplicate. Each of us has a unique set of talents, experiences, passions and desires that make us who we are.

Scientifically, we can see proof of this in the fact that identical twins in utero come out with completely different talents and desires—even different personalities and outlooks on life. One may be a tennis player with an outgoing, fearlessly optimistic personality, while the other may become a timid, intellectually curious, socially shy college professor.

Every experience we have, regardless of our chemical makeup or DNA design, informs who we are. Being bullied as a child might make us feel insecure, even inferior, while bullying others as a child might make us feel remorseful or remorseless. Kind words, negative words, fat-shaming or confidence-building can all echo through our souls as they continue to form and shape us, even wound and damage us, years, decades later.

What you hear at the dinner table each night growing up can truly echo through your life as an adult, so let's all hope it sounds more like, "Please pass the peas," and less like, "Whoa, I think you've had enough!"

Your Soul is a Blank Slate

It is never too early to imprint a child's soul. Think about a baby's birth. It comes out of the birth canal kicking and screaming, completely naked and vulnerable. As Tony Robbins is famous for saying, "It's the only time a fat, bald, drooling person gets picked up, cuddled and told they are so adorable." And that's where all the trouble starts!

As babies, we are completely dependent on our parents. They feed us, change our diapers and care for us. If they didn't, we would die. So we learn as babies that we'd better continue to get our parents' attention and love if we're going to survive, let alone thrive.

We are clever, too. We know that if we cry, that nice lady will come pick us up, and hey, if we cry long and loud enough, she'll probably feed us too, or at least get rid of that miserable stench in our diapers. But then life starts to happen. Stuff gets real.

We grow up, learn to fend for ourselves and even feed and wipe ourselves. Somewhere along the way, that nice lady stops responding to us the way she did when we were infants, and so we learn other techniques to get her attention.

Maybe we learn to smile, rebel, perform, get straight A's or study to be a lawyer—something, anything that will get their attention again. Maybe we learn to be the class clown, the good girl or the bad girl, the pretty one or the smart one, the thin one or the fat one, the happy one or the sad one.

Our Personal Evolution

As we continue into adulthood, we instinctively and inevitably learn which parts of our authentic selves have to be suppressed in order to earn our parents' love. Meanwhile, some of our true feelings and characteristics get pushed aside, maybe even suppressed, in order to fit how we think we must behave to get the love and attention we so desperately want and need.

We cling to the approval of our family and friends, our group, our team, our clique or our table in the cafeteria. We learn that the thoughts we have—the weird, the sweet and the funny—are usually squashed, mocked, questioned or used to alienate us if we dare share them out loud, so instead we morph into a shadow of our true selves and put on our "game face," the one everyone else expect of us.

Maybe we're more than just the smart girl, or the pretty girl, or the jock or the nerd or the stud, but few will ever know, because the desire to fit in and be accepted often overrides our desire to be comfortable with ourselves and who we authentically are.

As we continue to develop into adulthood, we realize that many of the decisions that shape who we are have been made, for the most part, unconsciously. Since we instinctively crave acceptance, our instincts and habits begin to flow in that direction—first consciously, and then subconsciously, by habit.

These parts of ourselves that we have rejected and are not even aware of may just be decisions that we made because, say, our father always wanted a football player in the family so we became athletic, or our mother hated being overshadowed so we learned how to suppress our outgoing personality, growing quiet and unassuming instead.

While each of our stories is a bit different from the next, the fact is that we often write it for the approval of others rather than ourselves—that is, unless we take the time, energy and effort to make a connection with our true selves.

Make a Soul Connection

Understanding our authentic selves allows us to reconnect with our universal right: *bliss*. It's there, and it's been there all the time—we've just been looking for it in all the wrong places. But what do our souls have to do with bliss? Well, everything. When we are able to live according to our soul's *true* nature, we are able to live a meaningful life of bliss.

In the yogic tradition, "yoga" literally means "union." In other words, it is the balance between our mind, body and soul. We have already explored the connection between our bodies and our environment, as well as that of our body and mind. Now let's talk about our *soul connection.*

As we become disconnected from our soul's purpose, we lose touch with our true, authentic selves, often leading to unhappiness and discontent. For me, this was the feeling that I was doing the "corporate thing" for my father, who above all valued financial success. I felt as though I was a Stepford Wife, programmed to be the "perfect woman" by a lifetime of watching this in my own home growing up. I knew all too well what my parents, in particular my father, expected of the ultimate woman, and I had been groomed all my life to deliver on that expectation, regardless of what *I* deemed "perfection" as a woman, mother, spouse, mate, employee or friend. I had ignored my own soul's whispers and desires for those of everyone else.

Not only was I supposed to be the perfect mother, take care of the kids, remember all the parent-teacher interviews, keep a clean house, get the groceries and prepare the meals, but I was also supposed to run a successful business and do it with a perfect manicure and a fabulous body. No wonder I was stressed, worn out, insecure and angry all the time! No wonder I felt less than perfect and more than frustrated. I knew my life was spinning off the rails and that I was out of balance, even out of whack. I knew that if something didn't give, I would surely break.

Ultimately, meditation is what allowed me to go inside and discover *who I really was.* Each time you access that stillness that's inside each of us, the "should's" can start to disappear. You know the should's…

- **I should be the class mother**
- **I should be more patient**
- **I shouldn't be so grumpy in the morning**
- **I should buy organic**
- **I should look like her**
- **I should really be at the gym**
- **I should bake those cookies for the bake sale**
- **I should stop going to bed so late**
- **I should be more charitable**

Instead of living up to what you think you "should" do and who you think you "should" be, you can ignore all that and do the soul work that needs to happen in order to find your *whole self* and uncover true bliss.

Your Whole Self

Our *whole self* is made up of the good, the bad and the ugly. Each of those parts serves an important purpose. The "good" girl probably got us love and attention from our parents and significant others. The "bad" girl probably had the nerve to stand up for herself and make things happen when we needed her the most. The "ugly" side probably couldn't figure out another way to get her needs met and simply acted out, the way we sometimes do when our wires get crossed and our sanity looks the other way.

We all do stupid things sometimes, simply because we can't see another way at the time. But don't be so hard on yourself; your whole self needs the good, the bad *and* the ugly to survive and to evolve. After all, how else would we learn and grow?

Who hasn't looked back with a blush or a grin at what we did in high school, college or last weekend at our cousin's wedding? We are constantly evolving, and to try to achieve perfection is a fool's errand. Better to strive for *wholeness* instead, which includes understanding—if not embracing—the good, the bad *and* the ugly side of ourselves.

Let's look at Bill Clinton as an example of a 'whole' individual. His "good" side got him voted into presidency of the United States (not too shabby, eh?). Not just that, but he turned out to be what some consider one of the most popular and well-regarded presidents of the last three or four decades. His accomplishments are too numerous to list but include working to combat world AIDS and campaigning against childhood obesity.

Clearly, his empathic nature and desire to make the world a better place are wonderful qualities. His "bad" side, however, was expressed in his anger. Among his staff, Clinton was famous for his rage. In the book *In Search of Bill Clinton,* American political consultant and former presidential advisor David Gergen shares, "Once on Air Force One, Clinton erupted so violently that I wished I had a parachute." And yet this intensity also led him to persevere. As Clinton has said, "I'm the big rubber doll you had as a kid, and every time you hit it, it bounces back."

And we all know about the "ugly." Clinton's escapade with Monica Lewinsky has certainly been debated publicly, and yet perhaps his desire for adoration was the only way he could fill his need for love and connection. Regardless of how you feel about his political legacy, Clinton's many traits and characteristics—the good, the bad and the ugly—are proof that we all have many sides to ourselves. The qualities that we choose to nurture and develop are our choice. And yet our dark side is not to be ignored, but rather embraced. If we can't love ourselves (that includes *all* sides of ourselves!) first, then how can we expect anyone else to?

Our soul's purpose is to live a life that allows us to express our true identity—not the identity that we feel chained to or learned to aspire to at our childhood dinner table. Sometimes the stories we tell ourselves regarding those qualities fill us with shame or remorse. Yet in our collective soul, the qualities that each one of us shares can be nurtured and developed to allow us to lead a blissful life.

For example, let's assume our soul's purpose and desire is to become a teacher. But our parents made it clear throughout our upbringing that they didn't want us to become a teacher. They thought teachers don't make enough money, or it's not a 'good enough' job title for their little boy or girl. They want a business professional instead. Wanting to be viewed as "successful" to our parents, and yearning for their approval and love, we neglect to develop that teaching side of ourselves. We bury it.

Instead of nurturing our caring, helpful, patient side, we develop the qualities of a good businessperson: aggressive, risk-taking, cunning, ruthless and shrewd. This is not who we *really* are, so inevitably we begin to hate ourselves and the life we've created as a business professional. Meanwhile, our authentic teaching side, begging to come out and be seen (and accepted), stays buried deep inside, creating feelings of emptiness and resentment.

But our bodies *know* our true feelings and desires, whether we acknowledge them or not. In fact, ignoring what's within will only do us more harm. Sooner or later, if we continue to push the feelings down and ignore them, we may start to develop or manifest physical symptoms from our repressed feelings. In some cases, this can lead to dis-ease, depression, anxiety… the list goes on and on. And who wants that?

In other words, many of us are out of alignment with our true path. We start to develop anxiety about our work. We can't sleep at night because of the stress and misery of our position. Our immune system may become weakened, or we may develop high blood pressure or inflammation, both of which can lead to heart disease or heart attack. These physical manifestations are often a result of a mind-body-soul connection that's out of balance. But don't fret—we can find that balance again.

So how can we re-discover our true purpose? One that allows us to lead our life in *alignment* rather than with *dis-ease*? Let's start with some self-inquiry to dig a little deeper and see what we uncover. Deepak Chopra says to ask yourself these three questions:

1. **Who am I?** *What do I value? What is at my core?*
2. **What do I want? What are my dreams, my aspirations?** *They can be material, ethereal, physical, spiritual… anything you would like to see fulfilled.*
3. **What is my purpose in life?** *How can I help? How can I best serve?*

Now spend twenty minutes just focusing on your breath. Breathing connects our mind to our soul. As we have dug a little deeper by asking ourselves some questions, we can now surrender to our unconscious and answer them from the place that no falseness, lying or fakeness can ever penetrate: the depths of our most authentic self, our soul.

Your Collective Soul

Now let's look at the big picture and see how our individual souls are intertwined with what some call the *collective soul.* Eastern traditions in particular teach that we have not only our own soul but a universal soul as well.

In Western culture, on the other hand, we tend to get caught up in our own drama. We become the center of our own universe, for better or worse, and other than a small manageable circle of family and friends, we tend to discount and sometimes even ignore the rest of the world.

From the universal perspective, our own stories are less important. Take, for example, the story of a young woman who absolutely "must" lose ten pounds before her wedding. She diets and struggles for weeks, trying desperately to take off the weight. She is determined to look exactly the way she wants in her new wedding gown. Two weeks before her wedding, war breaks out and food becomes rationed. Her abundant food supply is cut off and she is left to barter jewelry for whatever food she can manage. People all around her are starving, and now her diet and obsession with looking flawless in her wedding dress seem much less important.

All perspectives are equally important. We can't deny the importance of our own journey, but we also must recognize that we are interconnected with the journeys of others, often those who are less fortunate than we are. More than just a ripple effect from our own actions, what we put into the universe—our thoughts, emotions, energies, feelings—affect more than just ourselves.

Similarly, the human experience is shared. In his book *The Wise Heart: A Guide to the Universal Teachings of Buddhist Philosophy,* author Jack Kornfield describes a woman who stands up at one of his lectures in tremendous pain because of her partner's suicide. After working with her on compassion and forgiveness, he asks the room filled with 3,000 people if anyone else had lost someone due to suicide. Three-hundred people stood up.

Truly, there is comfort in our shared human condition. To deny the importance of others' experiences, or even to discount how their experiences mirror yours—or yours theirs—is to close yourself off from the healing powers of the universe.

Yogic tradition has a very inspiring perspective about our collective soul. In this spiritual realm, there are gods and goddesses that reside with one desire: *to express their creativity through us.*

All of the qualities that exist in each of us (the good the bad *and* the ugly) exist in the collective domain. All of the stories that have been repeated over the years, from biblical stories to Shakespeare, which give us examples of human triumphs and tragedy, belong to and come from that collective soul of experience, wisdom, passion and creativity. We can learn from these archetypes and examples so that we can create the lives we truly want to lead. We have the power to co-create our story with the universe.

In our quest to fill our lives with health, happiness and abundance, we can pull from many examples. For instance, I like to use Kris Carr, best-selling author, wellness activist and entrepreneur, as my personal archetype for someone who has faced adversity and managed to create a life of health, happiness and abundance. She has a rare, incurable form of cancer yet calls herself a cancer "thriver." Through her strength, I see potential; through her power I sense perseverance; and through her example, I find inspiration and support.

Think about the qualities you would like to see more of in your own life. Would you like more strength? Call on Zeus, call on Shakespeare or your own personal hero of choice. Find inspiration and support in the world, and look beyond your own front door. Ask yourself what type of life you want, and then find inspiration and strength in those who have achieved a similar style of lifestyle, peace, happiness or health.

We are all in this together—not just physically on this planet but spiritually in this universe. By realizing how interconnected we are, we can see how, by helping each other, we end up helping ourselves.

Activity: *Getting In Touch With Your Soul*

Now I want to share a mindful meditation exercise to help get you closer to your true self, your soul. This is something you can do every day or as often as you like, to reacquaint yourself with, well… yourself! It doesn't cost anything, it doesn't hurt, and if you simply try it once, I think you'll be hooked. But first you have to try. Here's how:

- **Sit comfortably and close your eyes.**
- **Start by taking a few breaths.**
- **Notice if you are comfortable.** If not, shift your position to get as comfortable as possible.
- **Now notice what is going on around you.** Do you hear a car alarm in the distance? The sound of someone taking a shower? Someone speaking nearby?
- **Try not to judge the sounds.** Just hear them. Accept them.
- **Now notice the temperature of the room.** Is it warm or cool? Can you feel the air on your skin?

- **Now that you are more acclimated to your surroundings and yourself, focus inward.** Are you feeling anxious? Calm? Angry? There is no right or wrong answer—simply notice your thoughts without judgment.
- **Allow yourself to focus on the breaths that you take.** From time to time, you may notice that your attention drifts away from your breathing to other thoughts or noises in the environment. When you become aware that your attention has drifted away, consciously recognize that your attention has shifted, and then bring the focus back to your breathing.
- **I'm not going to tell you how to breathe, but I *am* going to ask you to become aware of your breathing.** Is it deep or shallow? Stressed or relaxed? Just noticing your breath will change it in some way.
- **Now focus on your in-breath, then your out-breath.** As you inhale (in-breath), relax and surrender; as you exhale (out-breath), release any stress and frustration.
- **Do this mindfully for the next twenty minutes.** Whenever you notice that you are having thoughts, just say "thinking" to yourself and come back to your breath.

The purpose of this exercise is to find calm and peace through focus. The aftereffects should be a calmer, more focused and thoughtful you. Every time you need to feel more of any of those things, try this exercise and *come back to you.* Your body, mind and spirit will thank you.

Part 7

The Get Blissed 21-Day Challenge

So, now that you have a deeper, richer understanding of how your body, mind, environment, relationships and spirit all work together, it's time to put it all together to create what this whole book has been aimed towards: *bliss.*

Part of living blissfully is living purposefully, and that's why I've created the following seven steps, which are aimed at helping you add purpose and bliss to your life, step by step:

Step 1: *Set Your Goals*

Even when it comes to something as ethereal as bliss, setting goals is so important. In our quick-fix society, we've likely come to the understanding that bliss can be achieved simply and quickly—be it through a pill, a drink, a course, a seminar, a book on CD and anything in between.

While some of these may help, the fact is that we must be responsible for finding our own bliss. This means taking ownership of the process and doing the daily work that it requires. I know you'll enjoy it once you settle into a routine and discover how fun and rewarding the process can be.

The first place to start your "bliss work" is with goals. Start small, and then you can branch out into the bigger, loftier goals. A good basic goal for your first week could be something like, "I will make myself more open to these lessons by following my guided meditation in the same place each morning." This is a goal that's both active and habitual; it's something you can do day by day, and it will help you to want to *do* more every day.

Something like this is also a good goal because it's specific; it tells you what to do (make myself more open), how to do it (follow my guided meditation), where to do it (in the same place), when to do it (in the morning) and even how often (each morning). The more specific you are with yourself, the less room for ambiguity and confusion, and the less likely it will be that you flake on following through. Make clear, concise, specific goals that are easy to understand and follow through on.

Step 2: *Scope Out Your Hurdles*

The next step is to identify the hurdles. By recognizing our challenges, we can strategize and create solutions before the hurdle knocks us off track.

For instance, if you know you're not a morning person, that it's hard enough just to open your eyes and pour the ground beans into the coffee machine instead of the bread maker, then setting a goal of doing your guided meditation every morning is just setting yourself up to fail.

Being aware of your hurdles gives you the ability to adjust and avoid hiccups along the way so you can stay on track. So if you're not a morning bird, set a goal that's more realistic for your lifestyle. Perhaps it will sound more like, "Every day after work, before dinner and after the kids are done with their homework, I'm going to follow my guided meditations in the sunroom with a big 'Do Not Disturb' sign on the door." This is a proactive, personalized goal that not only acknowledges your hurdles but works around them to keep you steadfast on your journey towards bliss.

Step 3: *Replace Your Old Habits With New Ones*

This step is so critical to finding bliss that I can't say it enough. If you're in a current state of non-bliss, then it only stands to reason that if you want to find bliss, then you must unlearn what's made you fall out of blissfulness in the first place. You must learn to replace your old (bad) habits with new (good) ones.

For instance, if your current weight is a physical and emotional obstacle to your bliss, then you must focus on identifying and replacing the old habits that got you into that position in the first place. Let's say you move enough (exercise, walk, socialize, go out on weekends, etc.) but eat too much. Start by determining how often you eat. When and how much? When you're sad, lonely, angry, stressed or anxious? What types of emotions or foods are triggers for overeating? Once you become aware of your habits, you can get to work finding a solution.

By keeping a simple food journal tracking what you eat, how much and when, you may discover that throughout the day, it's not so much *how much* you're eating but *how often*. If you're constantly grazing and find that you're eating seven or eight times a day, that can be a lot of food, particularly with our out-of-whack portion sizes.

So maybe a goal could be to eat two less times per day. Sounds simple enough, but what are you going to do instead of eating those two times every day? Old habits are hard to break, but replacing them with something else can make the process easier. Maybe instead of eating one of your usual snacks at 10 a.m., you could go for a walk instead. And during another one of your afternoon feedings, you might consider going for another short walk. If that's not possible, try something else that's active or occupying to take your mind off the cravings you usually feel at that time.

It's not so much about doing something healthier at this point, like going to the gym or walking around your office building, but doing something new and different to get you out of your rut and into practicing new behavior. If you can replace the behavior that is making you reach for food two extra times per day with a different habit, such as getting up and moving, listening to music, reading a book or reaching out to a friend, eventually you will grow healthier by steadily losing the extra pounds that resulted from your previous habits.

This is not meant to be a diet book, but if your current weight or level of fitness are keeping you from feeling blissful, then you must change the habits that are getting in the way.

Step 4: *See the Black Hole*

Your "black holes" are your internal conflicts. These are what can cause you to sabotage yourself and any progress you make. What is it that keeps you from achieving your goals? For instance, one of my clients wanted desperately to lose weight. She wanted to be thin and beautiful. But having been abused as a child made her want to hide herself physically. And she did. She made sure no one would ever touch her again. She used food to numb the pain as well as keep men away, in an attempt—conscious or subconscious—to protect herself.

Pay attention to your internal dialogue. Notice the stories that you tell yourself. If you notice that your inner voices aren't in alignment with your soul's purpose, then practice the exercise on **page 45**. What does your limiting belief cost you? Your health, your social life, your self-respect? Write it all down. Now come up with your new story. See yourself as you want to be. Now practice, practice, practice. Don't be afraid to be active in your search for bliss, especially if it means jumping into the black hole that blocks happiness. Recognizing and coming face-to-face with your internal conflicts allows you to move forward and make positive changes, guiding you towards bliss.

Step 5: *Make Lifestyle Changes*

This is a book about change, and this step makes it clear: to find bliss, you will have to make some definite lifestyle changes. These may include things like:

- **Learning to manage your stress**
- **Learning new ways to eat and exercise**
- **Finding someone you trust to share your thoughts and feelings with** (even if it's just a journal!)
- **Learning to accept yourself**—the good, the bad *and* the ugly
- **Developing a support system**
- **Laughing** (sometimes at yourself!)
- **Cleaning up your environment as best you can** (this can mean no cigarette smoke to no clutter—whatever makes the most sense for you)
- **Making yourself a priority**
- **Learning to say NO** (and not feeling bad about it!)

Learning how to change your habits and behavior may mean making big, drastic changes, or smaller, more habitual ones—whichever works best for you. But regardless, change is in the air. I know this can be scary! Change is hard, particularly when you know that it's all up to you. It's easy, in other words, to *not* change—to slip back into old habits and give up changing and progressing altogether. But you deserve so much more than that. I want to see you thrive and enjoying the health, happiness and bliss that you deserve! If you follow these seven steps, make small changes gradually, change your behaviors over time and don't rush it, you will find bliss.

Step 6: *Have a Support System*

Don't attempt to do it all on your own. You need a support system to help you not only discover what's holding you back from bliss, but take you where you need to go to find it. I'm not saying you need a hand to hold every step of the way. Bliss is, first and foremost, a personal thing. Do what you need to do for and by yourself, but when you falter or get weary, having a support system in place will help you to not give up.

Make sure you have your support system established before you start your challenge. Let people know what's going on with the "Letter to Friends" we provided in Section 5, or something like, "Listen, I'm starting this new program, and it's different for me and I tend to give up after a few weeks. So if I need some help, can I call on you to cheer me up? Maybe go for a walk with me or just talk me through a rough patch?" I think you'll be pleasantly surprised by the reaction of most folks on your list. Most people will jump at the chance to be in a position of support, love and care. After all, it makes us happy to help and serve others, so why not give someone else the chance to be there for you?

Another option is to invite others to join you on the Get Blissed 21-Day Challenge. You can offer to be their support system too, so you can support each other along the way. Helping others is one of the fastest, easiest ways to bliss!

Step 7: *Reward Yourself!*

Don't neglect to reward yourself. It may seem like such an easy one to follow through on, but so many of us forget or don't bother to pat ourselves on the back. Give yourself the time, encouragement and support you need to find bliss on your own terms. As you reach each goal, have a safe place to stop, take a break and enjoy a small moment of victory. You can:

- **Take a weekend getaway**
- **Go out to dinner**
- **Enjoy a special treat**
- **Rent your favorite movie**
- **Attend a special concert**
- **Invite a special friend to dinner**
- **Have a relaxing "staycation"**
- **Buy yourself something nice**
- **Treat yourself to a massage or facial**
- **Try a wellness or yoga retreat**

Whatever your reward, don't be too stingy. Treat yourself often and for good reason. After all, there's no reason you can't enjoy a little bliss on the path to big bliss!

Tying it All Together

Do you ever wonder what you would do if life gave you a do-over? You know, the chance to learn from your mistakes and see what you could change if you could go back in time and erase certain decisions and habitual patterns? For me, that's exactly what happened on my 40th birthday.

I had been dating a wonderful man. We had just made the decision to move in together and try blending our two families. He had two teenage daughters, and I had two beautiful boys. My career was very successful, I had established myself within my community and I was dating the man of my dreams—everything seemed picture perfect on the outside. But on the inside, I still felt like a fraud. I didn't feel like I was "enough." I was still chasing financial achievement as a sign that I was worthy of love and happiness. I had no relationship with my brothers nor my father.

For my 40th birthday, my boyfriend threw me a party. My friends helped him coordinate it, and I felt incredibly loved. He also invited my father and my brothers.

At first I felt it would be a waste of time. Then I realized that it would only be a waste if I didn't approach the situation differently. If I went in with my usual victim mentality, the same pattern would perpetuate. So I switched my self-talk from "How dare they do that to me?" to "I love and miss my family. My children don't know their cousins, and I am hurting myself and my family by depriving us of the people that matter most. Holding on to anger is serving no one. Nothing unfair was done to me; I couldn't participate properly in my business role, but my role as a sister and daughter didn't have to change with it. My ability to give and receive love is still intact."

So I approached them with an olive branch. I hugged and kissed them and expressed how truly sorry I was for the rift that had been caused. I expressed my gratitude for them coming to help me celebrate my birthday. They were tentative but receptive. The old me would have been insulted that after I made such a vulnerable effort they weren't overly warm and welcoming me with open arms.

The new me simply took this as a challenge. After that initial reunion at my birthday party, I called and asked them to lunch. I reassured them that they could trust that this new me was here to stay. Slowly, inch by inch, they started to thaw. I basked in the warmth. One day it was no longer just me who always did the inviting, and I got to discover true, beautiful, unconditional love.

True love fills you up; it nourishes and supports you. It allows you to soar, take risks and flourish. I discovered that the more love I gave, the more love I got. It is an infinite loop of giving and receiving, and it is truly magical.

The day after my 40th birthday, feeling slightly hung over but remarkably self-satisfied, I took a pregnancy test. I was a couple of weeks late and had been told by my doctor that it was highly unlikely I would ever conceive. I figured I would check it out in the unlikely chance that a miracle had happened. When I saw the dot, I flipped. I had spent years waiting for that dot.

Now that I was no longer married, I figured that this was a cruel joke. I was a single mom taking care of two little boys. We were financially dependent on my business, and I couldn't see how I would be able to financially provide for my family. I worried that I would be judged for not being married. Then, once again, I changed my inner dialogue. I saw this as the true miracle it was: a gift from the Universe, an opportunity to make different choices, an opportunity for my own rebirth.

It was time to think creatively, to restructure my life. The first thing I did was envision the life I truly wanted. I imagined being home for my children after school, making them dinners and helping them with their homework. I imagined raising a baby and making that baby a priority before business meetings and travel commitments. I saw myself in a committed relationship where we could raise our children with common values and principles. I wanted to value myself over other people's vision of what I "should" be.

When I finally had a clear understanding of where I wanted to be, I made a plan for how to get there. I knew I couldn't just abandon my business, but I also knew that I needed to downsize, restructure and reprioritize if I truly wanted to achieve my new life goals. I decided to start something much smaller using the contacts, knowledge and creativity that I had cultivated over the years.

I hired people to do the work I was no longer able to myself and gave away many of the profits to ensure I had great motivated people around me. Then I took a leap of faith and decided to jump into the abyss, trusting that in the void I could co-create a new destiny. My old paradigm was discarded, and along with my baby, a new me was born. With each new challenge, I discarded my previous mindset and recognized that the only way to create a new future was to create new internal dialogues for my situation.

I went from seeing myself as single, scared and pregnant in an unstable start-up venture to a creative, courageous adventurer with new and exciting challenges to look forward to. The more I saw myself in this new light, the more my actions followed suit. When I faced adversity, I chose to see the challenge as a momentary setback, a puzzle for me to figure out. Instead of seeing myself as alone without a support system, I began to cultivate support from new sources.

My colleagues at work and I began to share responsibilities by helping each other out with school pickups, meal preparation and grocery shopping. Other mothers and I could take turns watching the kids so that one of us could get a much-needed break.

My wonderful partner and I decided to blend our lives more permanently and get married. I, who had felt so unlovable before, now had love coming from so many places. The love we shared had been just for the two of us, but now we were lucky to have so many other people be a part of that circle.

Looking back, I've come such a long way. From that dreary, dark, depressing winter years ago to where I am now, I feel like a whole new me in a whole new life. By using the tools and following the steps I talk about in this book, I was able to turn my life around and rediscover my inner bliss. This book isn't just theory, it's exactly how I got to where I am today.

I now have a life filled with more bliss than I could ever imagine: I have an incredible husband, five beautiful children, I'm surrounded by an incredibly loving family and I have a wonderful relationship with my father and brothers. If I could do it, just imagine what you're capable of!

The sense of purpose and gratification I get from my new life far exceeds anything I ever imagined for my life. I am truly blissed...

Made in the USA
San Bernardino, CA
30 September 2015